Meditation and Wisdom

禪定與智慧

MEDITATION
AND
WISDOM

Venerable Hsin Ting

Buddha's Light Publishing, Los Angeles

© 2014 Buddha's Light Publishing

By Venerable Hsin Ting
Translated by Jason Greenberger

Published by Buddha's Light Publishing
3456 S. Glenmark Drive
Hacienda Heights, CA 91745, U.S.A.
Tel: (626) 923-5144
Fax: (626) 923-5145
E-mail: itc@blia.org
Website: www.blpusa.com

Originally published as chanding yu zhihui (禪定與智慧)
© 2005 Gandha Samudra Culture Company

Printed in Taiwan.
18 17 16 15 14   1 2 3 4 5

CONTENTS

Acknowledgement

Like all of Buddha's Light Publishing's endeavors, this project benefited from the contributions of many people. We would like to thank the Chief Executive of the Fo Guang Shan International Translation Center, Venerable Tzu Jung, its Director, Venerable Yi Chao, and the abbot of Hsi Lai Temple, Venerable Hui Dong, for their support and leadership.

We would like to thank Yusha and the team at Gandha Samudra Culture Company for the cover design. Jason Greenberger provided the translation for the English edition, and the translation was edited by John Gill and Jonathan Ko. The book design was created by Xiaoyang Zhang. The manuscript was proofread and prepared for publication by Louvenia Ortega and Amanda Ling. Our appreciation goes to everyone who supported this project from conception to completion.

Chapter One

Beginnings

W hy do we sit in meditation? Why do you go on meditation re-treats? We do these things so that we can focus the mind and deepen our practice. We develop meditation to brighten the mind and see our true nature.

How We Think

We all rely on our six sense organs: the eyes, ears, nose, tongue, body, and mind. We use them to perceive and distinguish the six sense objects of forms, sounds, smells, tastes, touch, and *dharmas* (phenomena). It is through our senses that we become attached to craving for pleasant states, and develop aversion and disgust for un-pleasant states. We become led by our craving and aversion to the various states generated by sights, sounds, smells, tastes, touch, and *dharmas*. We ceaselessly discriminate, attach, and give rise to vari-ous aversions. Our minds lose the ability to settle down.

Within the mind we all have habits. When the six sense organs come into contact with the six sense objects, they give rise to six sense consciousnesses. At the time that this consciousness is formed, our habits react with these sense objects to give rise to various mental phenomena such as desire, anger, agitation, sloth, doubt, and re-morse. These negative thoughts become obstacles to our spiritual cultivation and meditation.

In a meditation hall the six senses are easy to watch over and protect, for there are very few stimuli compared to the secular world. There are five hindrances, five desires, and other afflictions that impede meditation that we must learn to let go of. Only by turning away from the hindrances can we cultivate meditative concentration, brighten the mind, and see our nature.

There are many methods, skillful means, techniques, and theories to help develop our meditation. During a meditation retreat, the monastic leading the retreat will provide the participants with

The Five Hindrances and the Five Desires

In addition to instructions on how to deepen and develop meditative concentration, it can be useful to know about the obstacles that lay ahead for a meditation practitioner so that we can be prepared. The Buddha called one set of such obstructions the five hindrances, which are 1) greed, 2) anger, 3) sloth, 4) agitation and remorse, and 5) doubt.

Greed or desire, the first of the five hindrances, is also of central concern in the Buddha's teachings. The Buddha taught that desire was one of the primary causes of suffering, and provided extensive teachings on how to identify and let go of desire. The Buddha analyzed desire in many ways, but one common and useful grouping is called the five desires, which is made up of 1) wealth, 2) sex, 3) fame, 4) food and drink, and 5) sleep.

spiritual guidance. The chance to enter a meditation hall is a rare opportunity, so we should approach it joyfully and with gratitude. There is no need to be anxious or feel driven to attain some level of realization. Meditation practice comes one step at a time. Those who practice meditation should put their worries aside and their minds and bodies at ease. In this way we can better focus our attention and skillfully respond to the environment.

When participating in a meditation retreat, one should keep the following verse in mind:

> The five hindrances and the five desires—
> Turn away from them completely.
> One can then brighten the mind,
> See one's nature and give rise to joy.

Mental Habits

We all have many habits. They affect the way we act, the way we speak, and even the way we think. An ordinary person cannot help but fulfill their habits, for they have not yet attained control over them. This is not to say that nothing can be done about false, illusory thinking. There are ways that we can gradually reduce illusory thinking so that, in the end, we can put a stop to it entirely.

The mind is full of thoughts all the time, so much so that it is hard to know exactly when it became so cluttered. The Buddha called this state "ignorance." At first, we are all like this. Consider the sky as an example: it does not matter if the sky is covered by white clouds or dark clouds, the space exists just as it is. In fact, the Buddha said the same of all the four great elements: earth, water, fire, and wind each have always existed just as they are. Just like we don't know when the white and dark clouds in the sky first took shape, we do not know when our thoughts and beliefs were first formed. Once illusory thoughts are present we mistake what is false to be true, and such thoughts manifest as unwholesome actions in body, speech, and mind.

We become attached to our incorrect views. These attachments to our viewpoints can lead to habits in our body, speech, and thoughts. These acts build upon each other, furthering our deluded thinking and meaningless behaviors, life after life, leaving marks upon our *ālaya* consciousness.

Alaya Consciousness

Whether we act in a way that is wholesome or unwholesome, pleasant or painful, everything we do becomes a part of our memories. For example, when we speak, whether we speak wholesome words or unwholesome words, pleasant or painful, all that we say becomes a part of our memories. This is natural. For each thought that we have, whether pure or impure, this too becomes part of our memories.

According to the Consciousness-Only School of Buddhist philosophy, everything we do with our body, speech and mind, while the action is occurring, is a *youbiao ye* (有表業), "manifest action." When these "manifest actions" cease and become memories, they in turn become part of the *ālaya* consciousness. The *ālaya* consciousness is like a storehouse that stockpiles all of our past actions. But unlike our memories, nothing in the *ālaya* consciousness fades away.

When a particular action is occurring, be it of body, speech, or mind, it is manifest—it's happening right now. After the action ceases it becomes a sort of energy, the same way that boiling liquid water becomes vapor. Past actions may no longer be visible, but they still exist.

Whatever actions we manifest eventually cease and change form to become memories. As our many actions permeate the *ālaya* consciousness, they form our habits and tendencies. Our habits, too, are a kind of energy that provides momentum for our actions.

If we were to use modern language to describe the *ālaya* consciousness, we would call it "memory." Whatever is most pervasive in our memories will manifest the most often, such as in our dreams.

The Eight Consciousnesses

In Buddhism, the conscious experience is divided and analyzed into several different parts so that the function of each can be better understood. The Consciousness-Only School of Buddhism traditionally divides consciousness into eight different types of consciousness:

1. Eye Consciousness
2. Ear Consciousness
3. Nose Consciousness
4. Tongue Consciousness
5. Body Consciousness
6. Mind Consciousness
7. *Manas* Consciousness
8. *Ālaya* Consciousness

The first five consciousnesses arise when sense organs make contact with sense objects, creating our knowledge of the phenomenal world. The mind consciousness distinguishes and perceives the information arising from the sense consciousnesses.

The seventh, or *manas*, consciousness is the part of our mental faculty that clings to the concept of an independent, separate self, and influences our decision-making to serve and protect the self. The eighth, or *ālaya*, consciousness functions as a "storehouse," containing all of the latent karma of our many, many past lives.

There is an old Chinese saying, "That which is thought of by day is dreamt of by night," which explains much of how memory works. The things that we say and do again and again in our day to day lives leave deep impressions in our memory.

Our memories help drive our decisions. If there is a person who constantly surfaces in your memory, you are likely to seek that person out. If you constantly think of an act, you will often commit the act. The same is true for everything we think about, from the foods we like to eat to the clothes we like to wear. This is how powerful the influence of memory can be.

Now we can see how our way of thinking is produced by our behavior. Every time we act, we strengthen that act in our *ālaya* consciousness. Life after life, from the distant past until now, thoughts are added to this consciousness. Many of our present actions derive from the thoughts present in our consciousness.

When we make contact with sense objects, we search our *ālaya* consciousness for memories. If we find memories of sense objects that are similar or identical to what we are presently encountering, we become very pleased. For example, when we see someone, we will think, "Hmmm... haven't I seen her before? Oh, right! I remember now. That's how I know her!" Just like that, we start to favor that person. The same applies to objects as well.

We can store limitless memories within our *ālaya* consciousness. As we encounter sense objects through our six sense organs we compare our experiences with our memories, developing preferences, attachments, and desires. What we don't recognize we often reject, attack, and destroy. As the six sense organs constantly come into contact with the six sense objects we develop greed, anger, and ignorance in our bodies, speech, and minds. All of this becomes part of our memories, and it is the memories of our most prevalent actions which guide us to the next life.

Rebirth of Consciousness

During rebirth, life arises in a new body. Though it sits in its mother's womb, a fetus's disposition, appearance, and health are not given by its mother. These qualities and traits are determined by the most powerful memories from its previous lives. A being who has generally made others happy and given them pleasure will be become a well-formed child. They will be born loveable, with a beautiful appearance, and have good affinities with others. If a being has often provoked the anger of others and brought people unease and suffering, they will have poor affinity with others and a hideous appearance.

Aside from determining the qualities of a person's body, appearance, health, and wealth, memories from previous lives also affect the habits we have in this life. As new lives develop, so too do old habits. Memories from previous lives play the most powerful role in determining what sort of job a person will like after they grow up, what sort of people they will like associating with, and other such matters.

In this way, our consciousness can be said to be have been built up from the results of our acts, speech, and thoughts over the course of many lifetimes. They will continue to collect, leading us to our future lives and so on forever. This is a powerful force which drives the mind. Whatever our preferences are in body, speech, and mind, all are conditioned by the strongest habits from previous lives. Even the slightest or subtlest of previous actions don't simply vanish. Energy cannot be destroyed. They are simply stored in our memories lifetime after lifetime.

The many habits imprinted on the *ālaya* consciousness can appear as stray thoughts when we attempt to settle the mind. Just as trees in a forest compete for sunlight, growing as tall as possible to outdo each other, our illusory thoughts are the same. These thoughts appear rapidly, one after another. From this, we can understand how thoughts produced by our bodies, speech, and minds enter our *ālaya* consciousness, manifest behaviors, and then become the "energy" of memory.

Threefold Training

If we wish to follow Buddhism in our everyday life, we must cultivate morality, meditative concentration, and wisdom. To respect others and not harm them, we must cultivate morality. To prevent unwholesome thoughts from becoming unwholesome actions, we must cultivate meditative concentration. To see the truth of the world and let go of illusory thoughts, we must cultivate wisdom. Only by cultivating in all three areas can we benefit both ourselves and others and balance both wisdom and merit.

The cultivation of morality, meditative concentration, and wisdom is essential to Humanistic Buddhism. In addition, we should fulfill the perfections of diligence, patience, and giving by trying our best to give sentient beings material goods, giving them fearlessness, and giving them Buddhist teachings. The task of benefiting sentient beings and avoiding harming them comes with many difficulties. We uphold precepts so that we do not add to the suffering of sentient beings by harming them through our speech and actions.

Many sentient beings are stubborn. If you treat them well, they assume you are using them. They will resist your kindness by insulting, slandering, or attacking you. Nevertheless, you must be patient. Patience comes from upholding precepts and cultivating meditative concentration, as well as developing wisdom. Only when one understands that the nature of all things are empty can that person calmly endure insults. Great diligence and practice in meditation is needed to develop the perfection of patience.

Aside from the perfection of patience, one should cultivate the other six perfections and the threefold training guided by wisdom. When practicing seated meditation during a meditation retreat, one must first spend some time regulating the body and the breath. Afterwards, one should contemplate their *huatou*, or observe the nature of emptiness. One must be sincere when studying meditation, and approach the practice one step at a time.

Chapter Two

THE ORIGIN OF AFFLICTION

As discussed previously, the six sense organs make contact with the six sense objects, giving rise to differentiation within the six sense consciousnesses. These interactions inform our physical, verbal, and mental actions. We can change our actions by cultivating morality, meditative concentration, and wisdom, and one way to do so is through an analysis of what the Buddha called the "twelve links of dependent origination."

Using our six sense organs, we can analyze our thinking and behavior. We can see the process by which our previous lives become our present lives, and what our future may hold. Through this training, people can learn why it is necessary to uphold the precepts, cultivate meditative concentration, and develop wisdom. Only through these efforts can we leave the cycle of birth and death.

Twelve Links of Dependent Origination

Within the twelve links of dependent origination, "ignorance" and "mental formations" are the deluded thoughts and behaviors from our previous lives. "Consciousness," "name and form," "the six sense organs," and "contact" generate the "feelings" we encounter in our present lives. Once we start receiving "feelings" in the present life, we develop "craving," "clinging," and "becoming." In our future lives, we experience "birth," and "aging and death." In summary, "ignorance" and "mental formations" are causes from our previous lives. Whereas "consciousness," "name and form," "six sense organs," "contact," and "feeling" are effects we receive in our present life. "Craving," "clinging," and "becoming" are the causes we produce in our present lives, and "birth" and "aging and death" are the effects we experience in our future lives. We cultivate ourselves so that we

Twelve Links of Dependent Origination

Past Life		Present Life			Future Life
Causes	Effects	Causes	Effects
Ignorance			
Mental Formations			
	Consciousness		
	Name and Form		
	Six Sense Organs		
	Contact		
	Feeling		
		Craving	
		Clinging	
		Becoming	
			Birth
			Old Age and Death

can control the links of "contact," "feeling," "craving," and "clinging." Only by treating these links can we eliminate affliction.

Contact

"Contact" refers to when the six sense organs and the six sense objects meet. There are two types of contact: "pleasant contact" is when we get what we want, and "unpleasant contact" is when we do not.

However, both kinds of contact are rooted in ignorance. Why? Within the mind we all possess a latent sense of self which we cling to. We think, "That's how I want to do it," "That's how I want it," or "I believe..." All these are products of our attachment.

Feeling

After contact has occurred, contact that makes us happy produces the feeling of pleasure. These feelings can lead to defilement, and to wanting to possess the thing, object, or place. Contact that we do not like produces the feeling of pain, which can lead to the defilement of wanting to reject, attack, or destroy the cause of the feelings. When we experience feelings, our ideas and impressions deepen, causing the connection between related thoughts to grow stronger. These processes shape our physical and verbal behavior.

Craving and Clinging

If these mental impressions become too strong, pleasant feelings will dominate our thoughts and we will long for them. This is "craving." These thoughts are an especially strong form of mental karma. The mind wishes to hold onto the feelings we crave (people, events, and objects) and not let go. This creates attachment, in which we spend all our free moments thinking of these pleasant feelings. This is "craving."

The power of craving becomes stronger and stronger, creating a strong sense of attachment in our consciousness, which affects our physical and verbal actions. This is "clinging."

Becoming

Clinging creates the momentum that leads to future rebirth. This moment is called "becoming." Becoming is fueled by all of the latent actions and habits stored in the *ālaya* consciousness. These impressions in our memory can be shallow and fairly weak, or very deep and strong. They can have a powerful influence on our future rebirths, but they will never allow us to escape from the cycle of birth and death.

"Craving," "clinging," and "becoming" occur in the world. As mentioned previously, our actions in the world can lead to good effects (positive karma) or bad effects (negative karma). Our actions may also not yet have the proper conditions for their effects to reach fruition, this is called "latent karma." By practicing seated meditation and entering *samādhi*, a state of deep meditative concentration, we produce only latent karma. This is because our bodies, speech, and minds do not give rise to thoughts or behavior in this state. This latent karma can bring us to the heavenly realms, and can be forged right here in the ordinary world.

"Contact," "feeling," "craving," and "clinging," are all part of "ignorance." Following these links, one to the next, will not allow us to break free from the cycle of birth and death. If we give rise to craving, clinging, and becoming, then birth, aging, and death will certainly follow. In the next life, one will give rise to new "consciousness," "name and form," and "six sense organs," which will produce "contact" and "feeling." "Contact" and "feeling" will produce "craving" and "clinging." "Craving" and "clinging" in turn produce powerful karma forces, but latent karma in our *ālaya* consciousness carries over in our future lives. People have always been like this, and will continue to be so, endlessly stuck in the cycle of birth and death.

Types of Clinging

"Clinging," one of the twelve links of dependent origination, can be divided into several categories:

1. Clinging to Desire

We have desire for form, sound, smell, taste, and touch. Desire is also often categorized as the "five desires" of wealth, sex, fame, food, and sleep. The pursuit of these desires is called "clinging to desire," and is one of the strongest forms of clinging. Society promotes the pursuit of the five desires. In some cases, people even steal or murder to obtain them. It is not uncommon nowadays to hear about a government official or a gangster being gunned down. Such instances inevitably arise from desire for form, sound, smell, taste, touch, and wanting the five desires of wealth, sex, fame, food, and sleep.

2. Clinging to Views

Attachments to thoughts, opinions, views, and philosophies can all be referred to as "clinging to views." Clinging to views includes political views. Metaphysical views like Monism, Dualism, and Pluralism are also examples of clinging. Differing philosophical beliefs can result in powerful antagonism, resulting in conflicts between different religions, such as that between Christianity and Islam. Similarly, Democracy and Communism have long been in disharmony, leading to global conflict.

3. Clinging to the Self

Because we are attached to our sense of self, we cling both to our own body and to sense objects with which we feel related. We constantly protect our sense of identity. This firmly maintained belief in the self has been carried through many previous lives, into the present life. After we die, we are certain to carry on clinging into our next life. This is "clinging to the self." The Consciousness-Only School locates this type of clinging in what it calls the *pudgala*, similar to the concept of the "ego." The attachments we form to our "self" create a powerful force that follows us through many lifetimes. Of all the forces that keep us in the cycle of birth and death, "clinging to the self" is the strongest.

4. Clinging to Precepts

When it comes to spiritual cultivation, some people may think one method is correct, whereas others believe a different method leads to liberation. Still, others may think that either method is meaningless, even though each group may hold to its own method as the only way to liberation. When one clings to an incorrect understanding of cultivation, this is called "clinging to precepts," and is another strong force that keeps us in the cycle of birth and death.

As these thoughts of love for ourselves and pleasant sense objects arrive, they are processed and give rise to craving, as well as clinging to philosophies, thoughts, and views. The way to mitigate and control the link between craving and clinging is to uphold precepts.

How to Conquer Affliction

Upholding precepts can bring the links of "craving" and "clinging" under control. No matter what method of cultivation one may choose, it is still best to adopt an attitude that is compassionate, respectful, and not harmful to others. As long as it does not negatively affect others, choose whichever method of cultivation you like.

There are some ways of thinking that, if we follow them, will cause us to harm others. The Buddhist precepts are designed so that, if we uphold them well, we will not harm others with our bodies by refraining from killing, refraining from stealing, and refraining from sexual misconduct, nor harm them with our speech by refraining from telling lies, refraining from using harsh speech, refraining from duplicitous speech, and refraining from flattery. If one upholds and abides by these precepts, no matter your perspective, you'll be able to avoid accumulating negative karma.

1. Upholding Precepts

During cultivation, the links of "craving" and "clinging" are the two links that are most likely to affect our behavior. They are the origin of most of our problems. We use upholding the five precepts and cultivating the ten wholesome actions to help be in control of ourselves. "Craving" is the pleasant feeling that we develop towards various people, events, and objects. These are the things that we feel "agree" with us, which is why we crave them in the first place. Since they are in line with our preferences, we often think about them. Every time we think of them, we strengthen the force of our mental conception of them. The memories connected to these persons, events, and objects grow deeper and deeper. As these thoughts become strengthened, so too does our likelihood to act upon these cravings.

When craving and clinging take shape as thoughts, we refer to it as "mental karma." When it takes shape as physical actions, we call it "physical karma." When it takes shape as speech, it is called "verbal karma." These are the three kinds of karma. When our actions subside and become latent karma, they form the causes for future ignorance and mental formations. Our various mental formations interact with each other and generate more active karma, which will eventually subside and become part of the *ālaya* consciousness once again. This latent karma will be stored until it manifests in the future due to craving and clinging. Thus the "becoming" from this life is a result of ignorance and mental formations of previous lives.

Craving and clinging come into being based on feelings from contact between the sense organs and sense objects. We uphold precepts to control how "craving" eventually gives rise to actions that create future "mental formations." Before our actions arise they develop in the mind for quite a while before they manifest. Through developing meditative concentration, we can have great control over "craving."

2. Meditative Concentration

Cultivating meditative concentration is often referred to as a sort of "preventative measure." A person well-practiced in meditative concentration can keep the mind clear as the six sense organs contact the six sense objects, and can know if their thoughts are pure or defiled.

We know what we should look at and what we should not. If we look too long at certain things, it will cause us trouble. In the same way, as we listen to others speak, but there are instances wherein we would be better off not listening. For example, you may misinterpret something someone has said, and come to think they were speaking ill of you. If you had not heard such words, no problems would have arisen. However, after hearing just a few words, you assume they are slandering you. Reacting to this leads to suffering.

If we can maintain mental clarity when the six sense organs make contact with the six sense objects we will be able to control our impulses. In order to do this we must cultivate meditative concentration. By using meditative concentration we can attend to problems when they are still at the stage of "contact" and "feeling," before they develop into "craving" and "clinging."

Why study meditation? Cultivating meditative concentration means training our minds and our hearts. This prevents the mind from becoming confused when it comes into contact with sense objects. When the mind is confused, it may give into defilement. We may give rise to greed for certain sense objects, and be unwilling to let them go. This can be prevented by regularly practicing meditation.

One major method of developing meditative concentration is *shuxi guan* (數息觀), "contemplation of counting the breath." Delusion arises when we are ensnared by pleasant and unpleasant sense objects. As they appear and reappear in our mind they create differentiation, deepening the impressions in the mind, causing behavior to manifest. This is when we should watch the breath. It doesn't matter if you count the inhalations or the exhalations, as long as you constantly attend to the practice. Choose to count either your inhalations or exhalations, and then try to do so for the time it takes to burn a stick of incense; all the way from the moment it ignites to the time it burns to the very bottom.

If you devote yourself to this practice and count your breaths attentively, you will become free of illusory thoughts. You can try it for a day or two, or if you are especially diligent, you can try sitting through multiple sticks of incense each day. Eventually, you will reach a point that your illusory thoughts come to a stop. With constant practice, you will develop this skill. After your ability to concentrate deepens, you will know when illusory thoughts arise and sense objects appear. This kind of frequent practice can bring you to a new level of mental cultivation.

Once we have reached this point, our meditative concentration will have quite a bit of power. The mind will be pure and clear. No matter what sense objects we encounter, we will understand and not be confused as we may have been in the past. No matter what we do, whether it is getting dressed, walking, eating, or going to the bathroom, the mind remains clear. Meditative concentration allows the mind to remain clear as it comes in contact with the outside world, as well as preventing illusory thoughts from developing.

What Is Ignorance?

Our present lives are conditioned by habits from previous lives, and are conditioned even more intensely by the sense objects we encounter in this life. Sometimes we may even realize we should not be thinking in a certain way, or that certain sense objects harm us, but we still cling, unwilling to let go. We enjoy seeing, listening, tasting, and engaging with various sense objects. Such habits are deeply rooted and difficult to control.

Imagine thinking about someone you detest. The more you think of him, the more you dislike him. Your anger will only grow. You know that continuing to think in this way will only harm yourself, but you cannot help but continue feeling angry. This is a product of habits of anger. Think of favorable sense objects or favorable people, and we will continue to think of them. This is why we sometimes cannot attain meditative concentration, because of our ignorance and habits. In the end, we may erupt angrily, shouting abuse at others or acting rudely.

We must strive to better understand our habits and the state of ignorance, which is mainly caused by a strong attachment to the "self." Dealing with ignorance is the key to treating our afflictions. "Ignorance" refers to wrong or false views from the past that cause us to see illusory phenomena and take them as real, including the "self." These are "ignorance" and "mental formations," which produce our physical, verbal, and mental actions.

These powerful karmic forces give rise to life, bringing "consciousness" to our current existence. "Consciousness" conditions "name and form," and "name and form" conditions consciousness. They require each other as conditions to arise. In this life, our present body is generated by "consciousness" and "name and form." As we are developing in utereo, our bodies give rise to the "six sense organs" of our eyes, ears, noses, tongues, bodies, and minds. Once we exit the womb and are born, these six sense organs encounter the outside world, and "contact" occurs, followed by "feeling." However, both "contact" and "feeling" have their origins in "ignorance."

"Ignorance" is nothing more than attachment to the self. As such, we always believe others to be at fault. Some of the most pitiable people are those who harm others without realizing what they have done. Because they are acting on their habits, they do not understand how their actions and words hurt others. They had these habits in previous lives, therefore they have such habits now.

How do we learn to be this way? The amount of "ignorance" we learn living in the mundane world is severe. We build on our habits from previous lives, making them even stronger. Unaware these habits are harmful, we fail to control them. We consider everything that we do, say, and think to be normal. This is why people harm others, think they are right, and do not consider their own actions. This is all a part of "ignorance." Wrong thinking and wrong views lead to harmful behavior. We may not even think our behavior is harmful, and thus do not see the error of our views. This is why it is important to understand "ignorance."

Many think that "ignorance, mental formations, consciousness, name and form, six sense organs, contact, feeling, craving, clinging, becoming, birth, and aging and death" are just Buddhist terms learned for scholarly research. Such people may say, "What about past lives? What about the present life? What I do in the present is where my future life will be." They think of it only as a process. But people who seek to practice the Buddha's teachings and liberate themselves from the cycle of birth and death approach the twelve links of dependent origination as a way to understand and improve their behavior.

Upholding precepts helps put a stop to the "craving" and "clinging" that has already arisen in this life. To prevent "craving" and "clinging" from becoming actual behavior, we must understand "craving" and "clinging" as they arise. Cultivating meditative concentration is necessary to gain control over "contact" and "feeling," for once these two links are under control "craving" and "clinging" will not arise.

"Ignorance" gives rise to "consciousness." "Consciousness" gives rise to "name and form." "Name and form" gives rise to the "six sense organs." The "six sense organs" give rise to "contact." "Contact" gives rise to "feeling." "Feeling" gives rise to "craving." This is the way to birth and death.   But if "contact" ceases, "feeling" ceases. If "feeling" ceases, "craving" ceases. If "craving" ceases, "clinging" ceases. If "clinging" ceases, "becoming" ceases. If "becoming" ceases, "birth" ceases. If "birth" ceases, "aging and death" cease. If "aging and death" cease, all suffering ceases. This is the way to *nirvāṇa*.

The ultimate goal in Buddhism is to enter *nirvāṇa* and become a Buddha. *Nirvāṇa* means liberation. The Buddha made a vow to "lead all ordinary sentient beings to final *nirvāṇa*, to cessation." This is Buddhism that is applicable to our everyday life, this is Humanistic Buddhism. If contact, feeling, craving, and clinging do not cease, how can we attain liberation? We should all work to cultivate meditative concentration, so that we can easily uphold the precepts in the future. In addition to cultivating meditative concentration, we must learn to see through delusion and let go. For this we must develop wisdom.

Chapter Three

BREATH COUNTING MEDITATION

Keeping up with the daily schedule in a meditation hall can be difficult. First time practitioners may feel fatigue, soreness, or pain in their legs and waist. This makes the anxiety they may feel even more difficult to bear. During meditation retreats, participants attempt to focus their usually scattered mind. Every day, from dawn till dusk, participants practice right mindfulness and carefully attend to their meditation objects. These are all forms of training. When but during a retreat can you spend all day meditating? Perhaps if you were to retire you could find the time. But, even then, meditating at home will likely not be as rigorous as it would be in a meditation hall.

Ordinarily, when the six sense organs contact the six sense objects it can be difficult to practice attentively. If you do not come to a meditation hall but instead opt to practice at home, it is easy to become distracted, thinking of this and that, and planning out your schedule for the day. Even if you are properly prepared and finished all prior obligations, there is still no escaping your own scattered mind. Meditation halls provide us with the ideal setting for developing good habits, such as attending to sense objects with right mindfulness.

Benefits of Breath Counting

Ordinary people habitually use their eyes, noses, ears, tongues, and bodies to indulge in external sense objects. Because of this, the mind seeks things externally. But by breath counting, we place our awareness on the tip of the nose or on the *dantian*. We can finally direct the mind inward.

Managing Emotions

Only by turning the mind inward can we find our original face. We can cultivate this habit of turning inward by developing breath counting meditation. All that is needed is a little time to not talk to others or be otherwise mentally engaged. When preparing, pay attention to your mouth and place the tongue comfortably on your palate. Pay attention to your inhalations and exhalations, and focus your awareness on the *dantian*.

By developing these habits, we will be more prepared when we encounter situations we don't like, like being around difficult people, and will not give rise to unwholesome words, thoughts, or actions. We can then recall our training and concentrate on the *dantian* or on our nostrils as we inhale and exhale. From this training we can gain a sense of deep calm and composure.

Dantian

In addition to the tip of the nose, another point to focus on during meditation is called the *dantian* (丹田), "elixir field." According to traditional Chinese medicine, the *dantian* is the central point through which the body's energy flows. This point is located in the pelvic region, about three fingerbreadths below the navel. The *dantian* is also used as a central point of focus for breath counting meditation.

> ### Original Face
>
> The Chan School of Buddhism is especially concerned with "brightening the mind and seeing nature," such that it has developed many similes to describe the process. One prominent simile for self-nature is *benlai mianmu* (本來面目), "original face." This is a paraphrase of the popular *huatou* question: "What was your original face before your parents were born?"

In meditation circles there is a term, *koutou chan* (口頭禪), "just words Chan." This refers to those adages about meditation that are frequently said, but not really thought about. In the same way, there are things that we are so accustomed to doing that we do them without thinking. That is why some people do not know when they do something wrong. Some people are easily angered. They will take offense with no provocation. They have a habit of using harsh language, and don't think there is anything wrong with it. But if we practice breath counting whenever we have time, wherever we are, even if only for a few moments, we will develop the habit. Then when we count our breaths we can be free from illusory thoughts.

Increased Composure

The instructions I give to beginners is to simply count their inhalations: Inhale, and count "one." Do not count your exhalation. Inhale again, and count "two." Remember, do not count your exhalation. Count from one to ten in this manner and then start over. Even those just starting out may be surprised that they have fewer stray thoughts as they count. If you keep working diligently and honestly, it will become a habit like any other.

Without developing this habit, people are easily agitated. Even the smallest infraction can set off a habitual bad temper. This is a lack of self-control. Just as a small leak can sink a great ship, a lack of composure can prevent us from succeeding in the future. If your practice of breath counting is well-established and you can maintain focus on the *dantian*, you will have greater self-control.

It is important to frequently train yourself. When you feel anger arising, shift your focus to your *dantian*. Keep your breathing steady to protect yourself. Prevent yourself from breaking precepts and harming others. Act with compassion and do not cause others suffering. You will be able to calm yourself down, develop a good temperament, and make a good impression on people.

Health

Once, a young man saw a co-worker taking his girlfriend out for a ride on his motorcycle. In his heart, he became envious. Later, that envy lead to jealousy. One day before the work day ended, he went down to the parking lot and let out the air in his co-worker's motorcycle tires. Then he hid far away and waited to see how his co-worker would take his girlfriend out now that his tires were flat. Not long after that, that co-worker came down to the parking lot with his girlfriend in hand. Seeing his flat tires, he began stomping and cursing. Off in the distance, that man looked on with satisfaction.

Some time later, that young man found a girlfriend of his own. He, too, took his girlfriend out on rides, and delighted in the experience. One time, he took his girlfriend down to the parking lot and saw from afar that both of his tires were flattened. As he got closer he saw that they were not flattened after all: they were slashed. His girlfriend became angry, but the young man remained calm. He understood that this was a result of his negative karma, and did not utter a word. Afterwards, his girlfriend told everyone that her boyfriend's temperament and personality were wonderful. Even after getting his tires slashed, he did not get angry.

If you are able to act calmly when encountering a problem, others will admire you. If you develop breath counting as a habit, not only will you be able to hold your temper, you will also be able to improve your physical health. By conserving your energy, you are less likely to be disrupted by joy, anger, sorrow, or happiness. Nor will you wish to have your energy depleted by the three poisons of greed, anger, and ignorance. Keep your mouth closed, rest your tongue on your palate, and become well-established in your training. These habits will help you in the future.

Stress Reduction

First, let us start by regulating our bodies. The physical, verbal, and mental aspects of our behavior engage our minds, our thoughts, and our consciousness. Our thoughts are numerous and scattered about, because they are created by the contact between the six sense organs and the six sense objects. In the modern world, we constantly see all kinds of different objects, with many shapes and colors. We hear all manner of confounding noises. Beyond that, there are all the things our tongues taste and our noses smell. The mind generates all kinds of distinctions, adding to this already complicated entanglement. It becomes impossible to put an end to all these illusory thoughts.

It is difficult to control these thoughts while exposed to the external world. The external causes and conditions we are exposed to are numerous and complicated. Sometimes your "to do list" at work is so long that your mind will be unable to settle down. Suddenly, you will start thinking, "I didn't do a good enough job on this," or, "I still haven't completed these tasks." People like this bear too heavy a workload. That is why they have so many thoughts in their head.

As the thoughts continue to pile up, they become immovable, exerting pressure on the mind. The mind begins to hiss and bubble like a disastrous science experiment, building up to an explosion.

In this day and age, we often live under a sense of pressure, feeling stressed in our day to day lives. Our circulatory and endocrine systems become taxed by the stress we feel. This manifests as not being able to sleep well and irregularity in our appetites. This stress affects our physiological functions and makes it quite hard to settle the mind down. Entering a meditation hall is an opportunity to completely let go and not think about secular matters.

The Basic Breath Counting Method

So how should we practice breath counting meditation? You can choose to count only inhalations and not exhalations, or you can choose to count only exhalations and not inhalations. You can choose whichever of these two methods you like. Place the tip of your tongue on the top of your mouth so it rests on your palate. The shape of your tongue in this position is similar to the position when pronouncing an "L" sound. This is similar to where the tongue rests when you are speaking.

While counting inhalations, when you draw a breath in, this is counted as "one." The following exhalation is not counted, and then when the next breath is taken in, it is counted as "two." In this manner, count until you reach "ten." Be patient with your counting, don't see it as boring. After you have gone from one to ten, start again from the beginning, and count your breaths once more from one to ten. Keep doing this for the length of one stick of incense. See how many times you can go without breaking your attention. How many times did stray thoughts arise? Practice frequently and diligently. This method seems really simple, but it is one of the most practical meditation methods of all.

The reason we have so many stray thoughts swirling around is that our six sense organs lust after sense objects. We manifest physical, verbal, and mental actions, which then become latent karma, forming habits in our *ālaya* consciousness. We may have formed the habit of letting our thoughts go wild each day, but, in the present, we can start regulating our bodies and breathing. We can focus our intent upon training in breath counting meditation.

When we sit, the body is not involved in other activities. In this posture, it is relatively easy to focus the mind on our inhalations and exhalations through the nose. This simple method helps to halt the production of stray thoughts. If you have time, you can try training for a month, half a year, a year or even two years, and you will find that your stray thoughts will gradually decrease. Slowly, your intention will become more cooperative when you call upon it to focus on your breathing. Breathing in, breathing out, breathing in, breathing out... stray thoughts will naturally cease.

No matter how many months or years we spend, if we are diligent, we will succeed in developing breath counting and enter *samādhi*, brightening the mind. Beyond this stage, practitioners can follow the path of wisdom to see their true nature. At this point, liberation becomes possible. Do not take breath counting lightly, even though it may seem rudimentary. If one keeps at it diligently, stray thoughts will no longer run wild. If you are used to counting exhalations rather than inhalations, that is fine too. They are both essentially the same: you still place your tongue on your palate and close your mouth. There is no need to be overly concerned about the length of your breaths, because if your counting becomes too rhythmic, the mind will be drawn back into giving rise to stray thoughts. This is why it is best to count either inhalations or exhalations, rather than both. During breath counting, if you divert your attention to the other aspect of the breath to do extra counting, you

---

Samādhi

The various qualities and depth of the meditative experience can be analyzed in many ways. The state of *samādhi* refers to a perfectly one-pointed mind that is entirely focused, lacking any distractions. Entering *samādhi* is a precursor to developing the deep states of *dhyana* meditation.

There are many different kinds of *samādhi* mentioned in Buddhist writings. Though they are all states of one-pointed concentration, they are often named for the different conditions which give rise to *samādhi*, such as "constant walking *samādhi*" or "constant sitting *samādhi*."

---

may give rise to stray thoughts. Of course you can breathe in and count "one," breathe out and count "two," but this method is used for other things.

If your breath counting becomes rhythmic or stale, it presents the same difficulties as using Buddhist beads to count recitations of Amitabha Buddha's name. Recitation may become habitual and rote. Even though the mouth may say, "Amitofo, amitofo," the eyes may dart here and there until you remember what you are supposed to be doing, and focus returns. Counting breaths is the same.

Other Breath Counting Methods

There are many ways to practice breath counting meditation. Some additional methods are listed below for readers to examine. As your practice of breath counting slowly matures and you are able to count from one to ten without any errors or giving rise to stray thoughts in between, you can relocate your attention to your *dantian*. When you breathe in, on one level, you will be counting your inhalation, but, on another level, you can direct your concentration to your *dantian*. The energy of your breath will naturally strengthen. This method helps increase focus and concentration.

Additionally, if your breathing is not smooth or the practice has become difficult, try changing your method. Temporarily stop counting inhalations or exhalations. When breathing in, concentrate on the tip of your nose. When you breathe out, concentrate on your *dantian*. This method can help the breath to even out, and then you can start counting breaths as you did in the beginning.

There are still other methods of breath counting. If breathing in focused on the tip of the nose and breathing out focused on the *dantian* doesn't help, try silently chanting "Oṃ maṇi padme hūṃ," the mantra of Avalokitesvara Bodhisattva, or reciting the name of Amitabha Buddha. While you should still pay attention to your breathing, the main focal point becomes the recitation. Your breath energy will strengthen as the mind becomes concentrated.

Gathering your attention in your *dantian* while reciting "Oṃ maṇi padme hūṃ" will deepen, strengthen, and empower your breathing, but the effect is temporary. It is a tool to make your breathing smoother; you should not always use this method. Wait until your breath is relatively relaxed, and then go back to basic breath counting, whether it be counting inhalations or exhalations. Just count clearly from one to ten.

After a period of time, counting from one to ten will become quite smooth. You will know that you can do it without miscounting. At that point, you can concentrate on your breath, inhalation or exhalation, rather than on the counting. Your attention can follow your breath, from inhalation to exhalation, without being fixated upon numbers. The beginnings of breath counting can be divided into these two stages: counting the breath and following the breath. Once the mind's attention can be completely focused on the breath going in and out without giving rise to stray thoughts, it is ready to enter *samādhi*.

The first two stages mentioned above are part of Master Zhiyi's "six wonderful methods." After "following the breath" comes the third stage of "stopping delusion." The state of "stopping delusion" describes when one is able to follow the breath all the way until entering *samādhi*. It is called "stopping" because the mind has completely settled, and illusory thoughts are no longer produced. This state is not some special method of cultivation, it is simply the culmination of the successful completion of following the breath.

The subsequent three stages of Master Zhiyi's "six wonderful methods" are "seeing truth," "self-reflection" and "purification." These three are all points along the path of wisdom. They complement the "sixteen extraordinary methods" of the *Anapanasmrti Sutra,* which are used to examine dependent origination, impermanence, and non-self. This is how developing wisdom can liberate us from birth and death.

The Stages of Counting the Breath

Master Zhiyi's "six wonderful methods" describe four different kinds of specialized breathing: bellowing winds, broken panting, low-pitched breathing, and internalized breathing.

1. Bellowing Winds

"Bellowing Winds" describes when one's inhalations become more and more powerful. As the breathing becomes deeper and longer it can become very loud. This is because, once the power of one's concentration has been gathered, it can be transferred elsewhere with great force. During practice, pay attention to the *dantian.* When your breath needs to be invigorated, inhalations supported by the *dantian* can produce surprisingly loud sounds. This is like how some people snore really loudly once the mind and body are completely relaxed and the breath has become even and rhythmic.

When first beginning to practice breath counting, the breath will be somewhat noisy; especially inhalation.

2. Broken Panting

"Broken Panting" is similar to when a child starts crying hysterically and then sees his mother coming. He tries to talk, but he is still caught up in the breathing of his crying. The inhalations have short pulses in them like the percussive "chop, chop, chop" of bamboo being split apart. Not all people experience this stage of pumping or panting in their breathing. Perhaps this is similar to, in acupuncture, the experience of opening the *ren* and *du* channels.

3. Low-pitched Breathing

"Low-pitched breathing" is similar to the kind of breathing used while practicing Qìgōng. This stage is not loud and noisy like the "bellowing winds" stage mentioned above, but one's inhalations are just as deep and long. One can hear the slight sound of breathing.

4. Internalized Breathing

"Internalized breathing" refers to when the movement of the breath has been nearly perfectly collected in the *dantian*. The breath energy feels like a melody, as if the breath is not even there. This is similar to the very long, quiet breathing called "turtle breathing" by the Daoists. Ordinary people have difficulty understanding the fourth stage, but if you are able to follow your breath smoothly and enter *samādhi*, that is enough. Perhaps it has to do with a person's physical constitution, but not everyone is able to experience "low-pitched breathing" and "internalized breathing."

In summation, when practicing breath counting, place your focus on the tip of your nose. Observe yourself and ask: When I breathe in and out, where does it go? Do I breathe in long or short?

Do I breathe out long or short? Are both short? Are both long? You should attentively look after your breathing. It does not matter if your breaths are long or short, just that you know them clearly. The mind and body are not separate. If a thought moves, our breath energy moves with it. If our breath energy moves, the body moves along with it. If you can link your concentration with the pulse of your breath energy, it is easy to get rid of stray thoughts.

If you concentrate on the length of your breath, and take good care of your breath, it will be easy to enter *samādhi*. Later, if you want to practice other forms of meditation such as contemplating impurity, contemplating skeletons, contemplating emptiness, contemplating the Buddha, or other such methods, the ability to enter *samādhi* will allow you to securely focus on these meditation objects. In the *Connected Discourses*, Śākyamuni Buddha taught breath counting meditation, but he did not ask that everyone count from one to ten. He just wanted people to pay attention to the length of their breaths. Whatever the method, I hope you are all able to make use of breath counting in your practice.

Chapter Four

MAKING PROGRESS

The Chinese Chan School has its own meditation methods, meditation hall layout, and style of scheduling meditation sessions. The methods taught by the Chan School are somewhat different from the methods taught by the Buddha. Each can be said to be on a different level. The Buddha taught a prescribed series of actions to enter *samādhi*. On the other hand, the Chinese Chan School incites practitioners to recognize their original faces in the present moment. This allows them to immediately grasp the significance of Master Huineng's verse:

Essentially, *bodhi* is not a tree.
The bright mirror is also not standing;
Inherently, there is no thing,
Where can it attract dust?

This is the exemplary feature of the Chan School's method for entering *samādhi*. It does not matter whether one is a beginner or a seasoned practitioner, the goal remains the same: knowing the present moment. For beginners, knowing the mind in the present moment is an opportunity to see their original face, with no wholesome or unwholesome thoughts. This is not an easy task. In fact, it is near-ly impossible. Even if a practitioner has learned to enter *samādhi*, having no wholesome or unwholesome thoughts is difficult.

The Buddha taught us that to cultivate we must uphold the pre-cepts, cultivate meditative concentration, and develop wisdom to-gether. These three make up what the Buddha called the "threefold training," and each complements and completes the others. In prin-ciple, upholding precepts comes first. If you are able to keep from harming others, your mind will not have any of the negative feel-ings of regret, shame, guilt, disturbance, or distress. After achieving this, entering *samādhi* is easy. This is why one must uphold precepts before training in meditation. On the other hand, as we apply our-selves diligently to meditation, the mind will become less easily ex-cited and agitated. Our behavior will then become naturally aligned with Dharma, and we will accord with the precepts.

Once we have gained the power of meditative concentration, we will be able to restrain the afflictions of the mind and purify our behavior. Once our words and actions are imbued with the power of meditative concentration, the mind becomes clear, and we will be able to understand thoughts as they arise. It will know the difference between wholesome and unwholesome, as well as the difference between pure and impure. Meditative concentration can also help prevent afflictions from arising in the first place.

Mundane Benefits of Meditation

Cultivating meditative concentration generates merit. Even if you do not practice the four bases of mindfulness or contemplate the three Dharma seals, those who practice meditation will still deepen their concentration. Meditation that makes one more focused, but does not lead to *samādhi* is called "mundane meditation." Mundane meditation has several benefits:

Four Dhyānas

The *dhyānas* are states of deep meditative concentration in which the mind becomes progressively more pure and refined.

- In the first *dhyāna* the mind has completely withdrawn from sense desire, but is still capable of searching and examining. The body and mind feel a sense of bliss and happiness.
- In the second *dhyāna*, the mind becomes even more balanced and peaceful. Searching and examining fade away, and only very subtle forms of thinking remain.
- In the third *dhyāna*, the mind becomes even more pure and blissful and develops powerful equanimity.
- In the fourth *dhyāna*, even subtle forms of thought fade away. The mind is perfectly still and peaceful.

1. Rebirth in Heaven

If practitioners can enter the *dhyāna* states, they can be reborn into one of the heavenly realms. After attaining the *dhyāna* states, one will be reborn in accordance with one's level of meditative attainment. In these realms, beings enjoy the results of their meritorious actions. This is regarded as part of cultivating merit and virtue.

2. Supernatural Powers

After entering the fourth *dhyāna*, one can develop supernatural powers. If one does not apply the depth of concentration one has developed to the three Dharma seals, the four bases of mindfulness, contemplative wisdom, and other such forms of right mindfulness, then all one's endeavors will simply lead to merit and virtue, not to liberation.

Supernatural Powers

While the goal of cultivating meditative concentration is to brighten the mind and see one's nature, that is not the only benefit of meditation. When the mind becomes focused and powerful it is capable of incredible things. The Buddhist sutras commonly name six types of supernatural powers that can arise from meditation:

1. *Heavenly Vision,* the ability to see through obstructions and past limitless distance.

2. *Heavenly Hearing,* the ability to hear across any distance and understand any language.

3. *Mind Reading,* the ability to know the thoughts of others.

4. *Teleportation,* the ability to travel freely through any obstacle and manifest any form or appearance.

5. *Knowledge of Past Lives,* the ability to perfectly discern the content of one's previous lives in all their detail, and how past karma will manifest in the present and future.

6. *Destruction of All Affliction,* the ability to completely remove the root causes of greed, anger, and delusion.

Supramundane Benefits of Meditation

Practitioners who keep in mind the three Dharma seals while meditating gain two advantages. First, they can enter into *samādhi* faster. Second, by regularly contemplating impermanence, the practitioner can easily rid himself of the five desires of wealth, sex, fame, food and drink, and sleep that arise when the five sense organs contact the five sense objects. By contemplating impermanence of all conditioned phenomena, practitioners can give rise to dispassion, let go of desires, and enter *samādhi.* Contemplating non-self also helps to subdue and control the five desires.

Three Dharma Seals

There are many different religious teachings in this world, so how can we discern what is truly the Buddha's teaching? One way that Buddha taught us to recognize the true Dharma is by applying the "three Dharma seals." To see if any teaching is the true Dharma, ask if it accords with the following truths:

- All conditioned phenomena are impermanent.
- All phenomena are without self-nature.
- Nirvāna is perfect tranquility.

When one has right mindfulness upon entering *samādhi*, one's behavior will be purer in nature. One will be able to uphold the precepts and avoid wrongdoing. Afflictions will rarely arise, and one will gradually eliminate his or her unwholesome habits. This is right *samādhi*. After right *samādhi* is established, practitioners can develop wisdom. The next step is to develop two attributes known in Chinese as *zhi* (止), "stopping," and *guan* (觀), "seeing." "Stopping" means to settle down the mind in meditative concentration, so that one can "see" dependent origination, and understand that the nature of all phenomena is empty, and that *nirvāna* is perfect tranquility. Once one is able to enter *samādhi* at will, this is attainment.

The first component of the Noble Eightfold Path is "right view": Seeing and examining the world through the logic of dependent origination: "When this arises, that arises. When this ceases, that ceases." All conditioned phenomena arise and cease. Go deeper and you will understand that all phenomena lack self-nature. When this is understood, you will see all phenomena as constantly arising and ceasing. They are illusory and insubstantial. One who has right view realizes that the underlying nature of the universe, as the *Heart Sutra* says, "does not arise or cease, is not defiled or pure, does not increase or decrease."

The point from the beginning stages of meditation to entering *samādhi* is the attribute of "stopping." Using the power of meditation to understand phenomena through dependent origination is the attribute of "seeing." These two attributes complement each other. The mind that constantly contemplates impermanence and non-self easily becomes calm. Just as one uses wisdom to practice *samādhi*, one uses *samādhi* to attain perfect wisdom. This is called the equal practice of both "stopping" and "seeing."

The Buddha taught us to uphold the precepts, cultivate meditative concentration, and develop wisdom. Those who cultivate meditative concentration for worldly gains, such as the desire for supernatural powers or rebirth in heaven, develop merit and virtue. Those who cultivate meditative concentration by developing the three Dharma seals and the four bases of mindfulness will give rise to wisdom. These two are quite different.

Meditation Objects

To practice meditation requires a "meditation object." A meditation object is an image we create in the mind to focus on. When we focus on an image and do not allow it to be disturbed or erased, that is a meditation object.

Among meditation objects, the best for treating stray thoughts is breath counting. Contemplating impurity is best for diminishing the five desires, of which lust is the most powerful. The Buddha praised these two meditation methods, calling them the "gates of ambrosia." As you develop your practice, you can learn to choose the meditation object which will best ease what is troubling you. To be chosen as an object suitable for developing meditative concentration, a meditation object must fulfill two requirements:

1. A Meditation Object Must Reduce Affliction

The lust between men and women is difficult to overcome. The sheer number of illusory thoughts produced by lust is overwhelming. In response, the Buddha taught us to contemplate impurity. This entails imagining a corpse going through the stages of decomposition, swelling, rotting, becoming worm-infested, and leaking blood and other fluids. Or imagine a skeleton. It can be a picture or even an animal's skeleton, just imagine the skeleton or the impurity of a corpse. Hold onto that image, fixate upon it, and do not think of other thoughts. This is the meditation object of contemplating impurity.

Another useful meditation object is the contemplation of loving-kindness. To practice it, imagine the face of your mother, exactly as it is. Make sure that the image is clear in your mind. Then imagine yourself sending her happiness, or healing when she is in pain. Use your power of contemplation to remove her sickness and replace her suffering with happiness. The image of your mother that you created is a meditation object for the contemplation of loving-kindness. Another meditation object commonly used to remove the obstacles to wholesome karma is to visualize Amitabha Buddha. Use an image you have seen (it does not matter whether it is a sculpture or a painting) to assist in your visualization. If you hold that image in your mind until it becomes well-defined and clear, then the Buddha becomes your meditation object.

2. A Meditation Object Must Lead to the Truth

Contemplating dependent origination, the emptiness of the self, or the emptiness of phenomena are all proper methods to approach the truth of Buddhism. If you take the contemplation of emptiness as your meditation object, you must ensure that you are doing so with right view. You should strive to turn all you hear into wisdom. By analyzing dependent origination and emptiness, considering them, and holding them in mind, emptiness can become one's meditation object.

By understanding that the world goes through formation, abiding, destruction, and void, and that all phenomena arise, abide, change, and cease, we will understand that all phenomena are impermanent and lack an independent "self." Knowing these things and seeing how they result in the perfect tranquility of *nirvāṇa* is to turn all that you hear into wisdom. To see things in this way is right view, and signifies that one has nearly completed their contemplation and realized *nirvāṇa*, though such a state is not easy to attain for beginners.

We should tend to our conditions and give rise to right mindfulness. "Conditions" in this instance includes one's meditation object. To give rise to right mindfulness means to establish single-minded concentration upon the meditation object. This is like using a rope to tie something to a pillar. By using a meditation object, you can tie the mind in place and make sure it does not fly off and become scattered. If you are not attending to your meditation object, the mind wanders and becomes scattered. If this happens, remember you are practicing meditative concentration, and bring the mind back to the meditation object. This is right wisdom.

If you wish to train in meditation, you should first learn the meaning of these terms. If meditation practitioners, lay or monastic, fail to utilize right wisdom and do not remain vigilant, they will not enter *samādhi*. Without right wisdom, you cannot be liberated from the cycle of birth and death.

Abiding with right wisdom means to maintain clear understanding as each thought arises. One knows which thoughts are wholesome and which are unwholesome, which are true and which are false, and which are pure and which are impure. One who understand these intentions can control behavior. One knows what should or should not be done, and what should or should not be said. This is why right wisdom is so important.

Before Samādhi: Nine Levels of Mental Focus

Usually, the mind is scattered. This is because of the interactions between the six sense organs and the *manas* consciousness, which generates ignorance about the self, views of the self, craving for the self, and pride in the self. Thus the six sense organs search outside, scattering the mind, so that it craves what is seen, smelled, heard, and tasted.

When the mind encounters objects in the outside world, it gives rise to feelings. Objects we want give rise to pleasure, and we think, "Can I get more of that?" This leads to greed, and if our needs are not met, anger. This is due to the *manas* consciousness' influence upon the six sense organs. The process is quite natural, and becomes a habit. Frequently, the mind gives rise to illusory thoughts. The most fundamental and thorough means to subdue these thoughts is to contemplate the emptiness of the self, see the five aggregates as empty, and weaken the *manas* consciousness.

However, before attaining the wisdom of emptiness, it is good to start by practicing within the phenomenal world. In other words, regulate the eyes, ears, nose, tongue, body, and mind. As Confucius said, "See no evil, hear no evil, speak no evil, and do no evil." In this way we should uphold the precepts to limit what we see, hear, speak, and do, and in doing so reduce our afflictions.

When you have time, sit down, close your eyes, and focus on your meditation object. Work to reduce your discriminations and lessen your afflictions. This is how one achieves success in meditative concentration.

1. Inner Focus

When cultivating meditative concentration, practitioners should first pick an appropriate meditation object. After selection, practitioners begin by collecting the mind and focusing their thoughts.

Concentrate on the meditation object. This is the first step in culti-vating meditative concentration, called "inner focus."

The mind always reaches outwards. A moment's carelessness and we can be entranced by external sights, and throw aside our contemplation in favor of external events and objects.

When the mind goes running outward, searching for external sense objects, it is an "unrestrained mind." Practitioners should not allow their minds to run wild. A practitioner should work towards forging a "tranquil mind." He should bring the mind back to itself; this is called "collecting the mind."

Once the mind concentrates upon a meditation object, hold it steady and cultivate right mindfulness. This is "inner focus." "Focus," in this instance, means to peacefully concentrate and fix oneself upon the meditation object. Previously, the mind was directed out-ward. Now the practitioner directs the mind inward. Locking the mind upon a meditation object is the first level of mental focus.

2. Continuous Focus

Cultivating meditative concentration is like adjusting to a new home. When you move to a new home, you have already grown accustomed to the environment of your previous home. Suddenly you are in a new environment. The people, events, and culture you encounter are all different. Naturally the mind will remember and incline towards the past. This does not even necessarily mean that your old home is better than your new one, simply that the six sense organs and the *manas* consciousness will cause you to long for your old home. The change in location is uncomfortable.

In the same way, in the beginning a practitioner is accustomed to allowing the mind to greedily pursue the outward world. If you ask it to abide inwardly and with tranquility, your thoughts may run wild. One moment, you want to go to the pantry to look for a snack. The next, you start thinking about your friend, politics, or the stock market. All sorts of thoughts surface. Some of these thoughts are appealing and cause a train of thoughts to build around them. You follow these thoughts for a while before remembering, "I'm in the middle of training in meditative concentration. How did I start thinking about all this stuff?" and just return to cultivation.

After a short while, our habits return and cause trouble, scattering our thoughts. This happens because the *ālaya* consciousness has so much stored within it. The *manas* consciousness also pulls strongly on these memories, making it difficult to calm the mind. When you discover that your mind has wandered, you should force yourself to return to the meditation object. Always bring your mind back into right mindfulness. Do your best to keep your mind fixed upon the meditation object. This process of bringing the mind back again and again to tranquility is called "continuous focus."

3. Calm Focus

After moving to a new home, you will often think about returning to your previous home. Causes and conditions in human existence are complicated. Sometimes, even if you want to go back, a multitude of causes and conditions tie you down. The mind longs for something, but you cannot do as you wish. Slowly, you adapt to the present environment and no longer reminisce about the past. Gradually, you become familiar with your new surroundings and make new friends. You come to see your new place as home. You think of the past less and less, and adapt to the present moment. This is "calm focus."

Those who have not cultivated meditative concentration find that the mind is constantly reaching for stimulation. When the stock market dips, their hearts jump out of their chests. But for those who understand that the world is illusory, cultivation becomes easier. The five desires and the five hindrances can be slowly subdued. The mind then peacefully abides in the meditation object. This is "calm focus."

4. Close Focus

Slowly, one's mind becomes focused on the meditation object so that it is always close at hand. In comparison to the third level, "calm focus," (often feeling homesick, thinking about the stock market, thinking about external pleasures) this is more advanced. The mind is less tempted by external stimuli. More often than not, the mind can be quickly brought back to meditation. The mind becomes capable of dwelling with the meditation object and contemplating past events. The mind remains close to the meditation object, and thus it is called "close focus." After completing these first four steps, "inner focus," "continuous focus," "calm focus," and "close focus," we are now able to completely focus on the meditation object.

5. Compliance

At this level you can fulfill the four right efforts:

1. Strengthen wholesome mental states that are present.
2. Develop wholesome mental states that are not yet present.
3. End unwholesome mental states that are present.
4. Prevent unwholesome mental states from arising that are not yet present.

The four right efforts are a method of cultivation that needs to be employed in your everyday life in order to impact your habits. The fifth level is called "compliance" because it is acting in accordance with the four right efforts. Before when you came into contact with the forms, sounds, smells, tastes, and touches of the external world, there was no resisting temptation. For example, sights and sounds of the opposite sex, or other pleasant sense objects, were irresistible.

A strong desire to possess those pleasant sense objects arose immediately. These are displays of greed, anger, and ignorance. These tempting sensory conditions stir the mind, causing the mind consciousness to discriminate, illusory thoughts to form, and the continued pursuit of pleasant sense objects.

After attaining the fourth and fifth levels of mental focus, the mind changes. Your temper will be less short and impulsive, and you will be more calm and serene. There will also be physical improvements. The mind and body will be relaxed amidst any sense object. At this point, you will have already known the bliss of meditative concentration.

Such people can experience the five desires of the outside world, but understand that sense objects only bring conditioned, temporary happiness. After the sense object has passed, the happiness vanishes as well. Additionally, this kind of extreme mood elevation later results in sorrow. In the end, happiness and excitement leave us exhausted. The bliss of meditative concentration is different. The happiness of tranquility has no unwanted side-effects.

A practitioner who fully understands the wondrous merits of meditative concentration would rather put aside the tempting sights, sounds, smells, touches, male and female forms, greed, anger, ignorance, and other external things in favor of the meditation object they have fixed their mind upon. When tempting sense objects appear, practitioners can use meditative concentration to control the five desires from engaging in inappropriate pursuits. They can regulate the body and mind, and comply with their meditation object. That is another reason this level is called "compliance."

All those who study Buddhism will experience this progression. They will come to know that meditative concentration can bring higher states of mental clarity. When the mind reaches this point of cultivation, it becomes sharper, clearer, and less clouded. This is "brightening the mind," as described in the Chan adage "brighten the mind and see nature." This means to make one's intentions bright, clear, and unclouded. Ultimately, all thoughts can be categorized as pure or impure. A bright mind can quickly differentiate between the two.

6. Quiescence

"Compliance" as described above shows how the mind can subdue the temptation of the external world, by entering the meditation object. By the time the sixth level of mental focus is reached, the mind is tranquil and has developed the strength to fully focus on a meditation object. When illusory, impure thoughts arise, one's concentration is sufficient to weed them out and eliminate them. At this level of mental focus, one can distinguish thoughts as wholesome or unwholesome, pure or impure, righteous or malevolent.

The last of the three Dharma seals states that "*nirvāṇa* is perfect tranquility." This can be verified by sages through removing all forms of affliction through meditative concentration. Someone at the "quiescence" level of mental focus can detect even a single unwholesome seed from the *ālaya* consciousness before it sprouts. One continues to develop the four right efforts, strengthening wholesome mental states, and ending unwholesome mental states.

7. Supreme Quiescence

The previous level, "quiescence" is the point where thoughts arise and the mind is attempting to differentiate them. It is still deciding whether something is pure or defiled, in-line or out-of-line with one's intentions. We consider, "Is this beneficial or not?" We are not yet able to simply cut off such thoughts with wisdom.

At the seventh level, "supreme quiescence," we are even more alert. We can stop illusory thoughts immediately, before they mature. When we attain this level, the mind is almost entirely focused on the meditation object.

8. One-Pointed Focus

In this stage, the mind is collected at a single point, and one's concentration is perfectly focused upon the meditation object.

9. Equilibrium

People who do not cultivate meditative concentration will experience wavering in their mood. If they encounter something pleasant, their mood will be elevated. When they are tired, they become drowsy and lose their wisdom. Such people are in a daze and lack equanimity. People who have trained in meditation to the level of "equilibrium" are able to preserve their equanimity and a balanced mental state. Their mind does not rise or fall, is not disorganized, and lacks even a small amount of confusion or dreariness. Instead, the mind is balanced.

After Samādhi: Dhyāna States

1. Entering Samādhi

Usually, we have strong thoughts of desire and greed. We feel unstable, as if we have massive heads and tiny feet. Our minds feel muddled. When we are about to enter *samādhi*, we will start to feel changes throughout the body. Our bodies will feel light, as though they are floating. Our minds relax, loosen, and gain greater freedom. We may feel extremely active. This feeling of energy begins at the head and spreads to lighten the entire body and mind. This sensation occurs just before entering *samādhi*. After this, one will enter the *dhyāna* states.

2. First Dhyāna

During the first of the *dhyāna* states, there are still some coarse and subtle thoughts present. The mind is able to remain pure and clear amidst these thoughts, but there is still progress to be made.

Once one surpasses the first *dhyāna* and attains the second *dhyāna* coarse thoughts no longer arise, but certain kinds of subtle thoughts persist. One will be completely focused upon the meditation object, though pleasant and unpleasant feelings still arise. This is the "intermediate *dhyāna*," a state between the first and second *dhyānas*, in which there is still differentiation between coarse and subtle thought.

3. The Second through Fourth Dhyānas

After entering the second *dhyāna*, even subtle thoughts cease. The first *dhyāna* is also called "*samādhi* with searching and examining," while the intermediate *dhyāna* lacks "searching," and is called "*samādhi* without searching with examining." The second *dhyāna*, lacking both, is called "*samādhi* without searching and examining." *Samādhi* is the Sanskrit word for "right meditative concentration."

If one continues to the third and fourth *dhyānas*, then the meditative concentration from the fourth *dhyāna* can be used to contemplate "the ten universal visualizations" (visualizing earth, water, fire, wind, blue, yellow, red, white, space, consciousness, and other such elements filling the universe). After one has completed this level of cultivation, one can develop supernatural powers. If this meditative concentration is used to contemplate dependent origination, practitioners can attain enlightenment and gain liberation.

Understanding the "nine stages of mental focus," you should select whatever meditation object suits your needs. Contemplating impurity and breath counting are the two "gates of ambrosia" that the Buddha left us. Breath counting is the most fundamental and powerful object of meditation. Contemplating impurity requires imagination. If the mind is full of scattered, illusory thoughts, you can hardly perform any kind of meditation.

Chapter Five

OTHER METHODS

All Buddhists, whether monastics or lay Buddhists, should cultivate meditative concentration. The only difference between the two is that monastics have a lifestyle that is better for training in meditative concentration than laypeople, and thus they are more able to succeed in their cultivation. Some may have read in the Buddhist sutras about a type of enlightened person called an "*arhat* liberated through wisdom," and cite it as proof that meditation is not necessary for attaining enlightenment. But an "*arhat* liberated through wisdom" would continue to train in meditative concentration, even after attaining liberation.

Our daily lives are filled with greed, resentment, jealousy, and dissatisfaction. These mental states must be removed before we can enter *samādhi*. After entering the first *dhyāna*, these mental states are subdued. Practitioners who have completely conquered these mental states are called "arhats liberated through both wisdom and concentration." "Arhats liberated through wisdom" take the development of wisdom as their main endeavor, but for "arhats liberated through both wisdom and concentration" meditative concentration is cultivated as well.

Entering into *samādhi* is quite easy for "arhats liberated through wisdom." They know that all worldly phenomena are impermanent, lack an independent self, and are illusory. Therefore they have no attachments. The fundamental conditions for training in meditative concentration are being without worldly attachments, without defilement, and without craving. These conditions are necessary for success in meditation. These days, Buddhism has been influenced by the Pure Land, Chan, and Esoteric schools, such that the need for these requirements is even more evident.

Meditative concentration is highly emphasized in the Esoteric School. For example, the final part of Je Tsongkhapa Rinpoche's *Great Treatise on the Stages of the Path to Enlightenment* is focused on stopping and seeing meditation. This is unlike the Pure Land School, which emphasizes relying upon reciting Amitabha Buddha's name. If the Chan and Pure Land schools practiced according to the methods taught by founding masters, perhaps Buddhism would be stronger. The Pure Land School probably emphasizes reciting Amitābha Buddha's name so that it can be universal, but their meditative concentration falls behind others.

Practitioners who want to use the Buddha's teachings in their daily lives must develop skillful meditation. Furthermore, they must have understood a certain level of the Buddha's teaching, such that all they hear becomes wisdom. Those who know how to contemplate the emptiness of dependent origination and understand that the world is impermanent and non-self can see the causes and conditions before them as impermanent, so that the mind can let go.

Consider if I were to pound my hand upon a table. My hand is the primary cause, the table is a condition, and the sound that is produced when the two crash together is the effect. Cause plus condition leads to effect. All of our ordinary matters depend on causes and conditions as well—this is reality. If we regularly cultivate stopping and seeing meditation in our everyday lives, we don't need to visit a meditation hall. If this were not the case, then we could only practice in a meditation hall from morning until night. The Buddha's teachings on meditative concentration was based around the five contemplations: impurity, loving-kindness and compassion, causes and conditions, counting the breath, and the Buddha. However, in Chinese Buddhism, chanting Amitābha Buddha's name and utilizing *huatou* training has become extremely popular. In the following paragraphs, the various methods of chanting the Buddha's name and contemplating the Buddha will be discussed. So will the methods of *huatou* training.

Hindrances and Obstacles

In the outside world we are faced with desire for sense objects, such as sights, sounds, smells, tastes, and touches, as well as the five desires of wealth, sex, fame, food and drink, and sleep. These all easily excite the mind and create worries. Within a meditation hall, we can distance ourselves from such sensory conditions. Therefore, meditation halls are the best environment for cultivating meditative concentration. Removing the five hindrances of greed, anger, sloth, agitation and remorse, and doubt and distancing oneself from the five desires are actually the same endeavor.

1. Greed and Anger

Greed and anger cannot be separated from each other. Anger is wanting what you cannot have, or having something you feel belongs to you taken away or damaged. When such things happen, the mind gives rise to anger. As greed strengthens, anger does too. Distance yourself from the five desires, and anger goes away. The best way to deal with the five desires is to be content. Those who are content are satisfied. It has no greed, and therefore produces no anger.

Consequently, cultivators of the Way should be content with their everyday environment. Our bodies may live alongside others and our minds may engage with society, we should try to distance ourselves from worldly affairs. Such things bring us away from the path, and are best put aside. An individual's body need not separate from the group, but one's mind should become detached from the group mind. In a meditation hall, everyone can single-mindedly apply themselves to training in meditative concentration. Without any conflicts or anger, it is easier to feel gratitude and understand contentment. A meditation hall is a far more suitable place for cultivation than the outside world.

2. Jealousy and Arrogance

In the world there are a lot of questions, problems, and opinions that come between people. This is normal. Among human emotions, the most visible afflictions are jealousy and arrogance. The two are actually the same, they just manifest differently. Arrogance is the feeling that you are better than others. When you see other people who are superior and enjoy greater popularity, the mind becomes unhappy and jealous. The Buddha's teachings refer to this as, "being intolerant of another's glory." Jealousy and arrogance come together. Even for cultivators, they arise often. We should consistently check ourselves for jealousy and arrogance.

The Buddha often advises us to find gladness in the joy and merit of others. This is to relieve the condition of jealousy. Jealousy can be the first step of even greater affliction. Next, one may try to punish or destroy the object of jealousy. As one becomes more jealous, afflictions become stronger. Eventually, this can even result in murder. Jealousy can manifest at any time. This is why one should turn away from jealousy and let go of the five desires.

3. Agitation and Remorse, Sloth, and Doubt

As soon as we come across a person, activity, or thing we like the mind becomes extremely impulsive and excited. Even during meditation, we will keep thinking about them. If we think about them for too long, it becomes impossible to return to the object of meditation. This prevents us from developing meditative concentration. In the Buddha's teachings, this impulsive excitement is known as "agitation and remorse."

If an object is not moved by causes and conditions, not acted upon by the outside world, nor blown along by the wind, naturally it will be still. If we can control the body and mind, our thoughts too will be still. We must practice for a long time before we develop meditative concentration such that no thoughts arise.

If the mind is filled with doubts like, "Am I practicing the right method?" "Is it working?" or "Am I in accordance with the Dharma?" your progress will be impeded. Confidence can combat indecisiveness. Acknowledge that, of the many methods available, cultivating meditative concentration is the fastest, most efficient, and most effective method to brighten the mind.

Agitation and remorse are linked together. The two are the opposite of the hindrance of sloth. A slothful mind may drift off into sleep soon after beginning meditation, such that no improvement takes place. Only when the mind is focused upon a meditation object is there progress. However, even after progress has been made, the meditation object may dissipate or become indistinct. If the mind has no power or is unable to focus, this is sloth.

A meditation object dissipates when one lacks the means to clarify or solidify it. This is a serious impediment for meditative concentration. Why are some practitioners unable to see their meditation objects with clarity? Because the mind is clouded by ignorance and afflictions big and small. That is why the meditation object may be unclear and indistinct. Unless you work diligently to clarify the meditation object, you will remain slothful, unable to enter *dhyāna*.

4. Disadvantages of a Scattered Mind

There are many benefits to cultivating meditative concentration. For laypeople, it can remove scattered thoughts and greed. In order to provide for their families, it is inevitable that laypeople pursue wealth, fame, and gain. However, if sought too hard, these produce great suffering. Meditative concentration can be used to satiate these urges. The cultivation of meditative concentration must be used to treat this insatiability. Only people who understand contentment can succeed in tranquil abiding. They enjoy a constant sense of happiness and freedom.

A scattered mind brings suffering. When the mind is scattered, it becomes difficult to do, say, or discuss things. A scattered mind becomes overly emotional and unable to concentrate. One will do or say things that one will regret, leading to vexation, suffering, and various regrets. This problem is frequently experienced by people with scattered minds. It causes them great suffering.

It is difficult to calm the mind while working. We are swamped with work every day, unable to discern the importance or urgency of a task. This is because we have no means of deciding what should be done first. Consequently, nothing is completed. For laypeople, the most important goal is to rid oneself of scattered thoughts. For practitioners who are still students, there is often little time to do so. Students should make the best use of their time in the mornings and evening to cultivate meditative concentration.

5. The Five Contemplations

Every form of affliction has a corresponding treatment, that allows us to enter *samādhi*. The five most commonly used treatments are called the "the five contemplations." The Buddha taught us to treat the affliction of a scattered mind with "the contemplation of counting the breath." Aside from this, minds heavy with greed, the five desires, or lust should be treated with "the contemplation of impurity."

The four forms of right mindfulness are to "contemplate the body as impure," "contemplate feelings as suffering," "contemplate the mind as impermanent," and "contemplate phenomena as non-self." Contemplating the body as impure is done to understand the interior and exterior of one's own body to both be impure and gravely polluted. It should not be confused with "the contemplation of impurity" from the "the five contemplations", which examines the stages of a decomposing corpse (the out-flowing of blood and other liquids, rotting, being devoured by insects, and so on) in order to elicit a mindset of wholesome fear and loathing. It is the most powerful method to remove the lust of men and women.

When Śākyamuni Buddha still resided in this world, there had already been cases where, after cultivating "the contemplation of impurity", some disciples detested their bodies so much they committed suicide or asked others to kill them. Afterwards, practitioners generally focused on one of two approaches: the contemplation of counting the breath or the contemplation of impurity. With regards to impurity, the object of contemplation shifted over time from "a rotting corpse" to "a white skeleton." With the latter contemplation, the bones are contemplated until they stabilize and emit light. This is an effective method for controlling lust, but the contemplation of a rotting corpse remains the most effective in treating the lust of men and women.

For treating delusion, cultivate "the contemplation of causes and conditions." If one is arrogant, cultivate "the contemplation of individual elements." In this contemplation, imagine your body separated into bones, muscles, blood, body-heat, breath, and other such physical phenomena as categorized into the elements of earth, water, fire, and wind. Sentient beings burdened by numerous karmic obstacles, can use "the contemplation of the Buddha." Reciting the name of Amitabha Buddha can dissolve karmic obstacles, while upholding mantras can cure illnesses. Reciting the name of Avalokiteśvara Bodhisattva also helps.

After you become proficient at counting breaths, try reciting the Buddha's name at the same time. While breathing in, you can recite "Nā mó ā mí tuó fó, nā mó ā mí tuó fó..." until the inhalation is complete. You can do the same for breathing out, repeat "Nā mó ā mí tuó fó, nā mó ā mí tuó fó..." Following this method of reciting while breathing can allow you to easily enter the *samādhi* of contemplating the Buddha.

Reciting Amitābha Buddha's Name

Different Buddhist schools will either emphasize the perspective of emptiness or the perspective of existence. For example, schools that study the perfection of wisdom teachings analyze the nature of worldly phenomena as empty, unreal, and lacking any intrinsic nature. This is the "emptiness" perspective. On the other hand, the Consciousness-Only School states that "the three realms are mind-only, and all phenomena are consciousness-only." They see everything in the external world as a manifestation of people's minds. It is through clinging to these images that they gain an actual presence and take on true existence. This is the "existence" perspective. One approach is to analyze the intrinsic nature of things, while the other is to analyze the phenomenal existence of things. These two perspectives complement each other. They are not meant to be in conflict.

1. Karma and Rebirth

When some people hear about emptiness, how all things lack an intrinsic nature, are made up of causes and conditions, and that there is no "self," they think "If this is true, then how can anyone be reborn into a Pure Land?" Answering this question requires some explanation.

The Pure Land School has been able to welcome everyone, whether they have a deep or shallow capacity for spiritual practice. Pure Land practice focuses much on those who have only a slight inclination towards spiritual practice: they are taught to recite Amitābha Buddha's name. By reciting the name, practitioners try to focus the mind and enter the *samādhi* of contemplating the Buddha. In this way, one contemplates the Buddha simply by reciting Amitābha Buddha's name and bowing before the Buddha's image.

Reciting the Buddha's name generates wholesome verbal and mental karma. Bowing before the Buddha generates wholesome physical karma. These three forms of karma are all conditioned phenomena; they are not "unconditioned phenomena" like attaining enlightenment or understanding emptiness. These methods rely on reciting the Buddha's name and paying homage to ensure rebirth in the Pure Land. But, it is not as if only one's wholesome karma is reborn in the Pure Land. It is certainly not the case that the wholesome karma goes to the Pure Land, but unwholesome karma does not. People bring their unwholesome karma with them, and must continue to practice.

For those with intermediate spiritual capacity, the Pure Land School teaches a system of meditative visualization to practice when contemplating the Buddha. This is done in two ways. The first is to look upon an image of Amitābha Buddha until you can picture Amitābha Buddha's benevolent countenance in your mind. Continue to develop this visualization until you can see Amitābha Buddha's body complete with all its details. Visualizing in this way will allow Amitābha Buddha to appear before your very eyes, such that one enters the *samādhi* of contemplating the Buddha. This is called "contemplating the form of the Buddha." The second method can be used without a Buddha image to look at. Instead, you visualize the sixteen images mentioned in the *Contemplation Sutra*. These images are the fulfillment of Amitābha Buddha's vows: the lush scenery of the Pure Land. This is called "contemplating the Buddha in the mind."

Training in meditative concentration leads to rebirth in the heavenly realms. This is because it mends the scattered mind. It only takes a little bit of meditative power together with upholding the precepts and doing wholesome deeds to be reborn in a heavenly realm. If you can enter any of the *dhyāna* states, you will leave the five desires, the five hindrances, and all male or female lust. The higher heavenly realms, called the "*dhyāna* heavens" can be reached depending on what level of *dhyāna* one can regularly attain.

As one's contemplation progresses, one reaches a state of single-minded clarity in which actions, words, and thoughts are tranquil and still. This produces "neutral karma," which is neither wholesome nor unwholesome. If you attain a mind this still and single-mindedly vow to be reborn in the Pure Land, you really can be born in the Western Pure Land of Ultimate Bliss. This is attaining rebirth through the power of meditative concentration. In this way, one does not attain rebirth through wisdom.

When you arrive in the Pure Land, your lotus opens and you see Amitābha Buddha, it is still necessary to practice the Noble Eightfold Path and the thirty-seven practices to enlightenment. We still must develop wisdom. This includes five faculties, five powers, seven factors of awakening, the Noble Eightfold Path, and the other items mentioned in the *Amitābha Sutra*. After your lotus opens and you see Amitābha Buddha, you awaken to the "patience of the non-arising of phenomena." This is the incredible patience that comes from understanding that the nature of all things is emptiness and non-self. When you have this level of patience, you are liberated.

Practitioners with an intermediate spiritual capacity tend to take meditative concentration as their main focus. They favor contemplating the Buddha in the mind, and practice the sixteen visualizations details in the *Contemplation Sutra*. Of course, it is also necessary to give rise to the *bodhi* mind, maintain compassion, avoid killing living beings, and uphold the triple refuge, five precepts, and all other wholesome practices. Practitioners of the highest spiritual capacity practice "contemplation of the Buddha's true form." I will discuss this method of practice later. Those who are beginning their study of Buddhism should start with reciting the Buddha's name to develop a fundamental level of meditative concentration. Afterwards, they can move on to other methods of contemplating the Buddha.

2. The Power of a Buddha's Name

When we utter a phrase, it carries a certain power. Just a few words can ignite a person's anger or influence a person's whole life. In Esoteric Buddhism, there is a particular wealth deity called "yellow jambhala," which is commonly depicted holding a rodent-like creature who emits treasure. Within Esoteric Buddhism, this deity is prayed to for blessings, while outside of Esoteric Buddhism, this creature is seen as encouragement for people to improve, advance, and work diligently. The two approaches are quite different.

Once upon a time, in the year of the rat, there was a young man who had grown lazy since his father passed away. After he spent his inheritance, he begged for money from his uncle. Compassionate at heart, the uncle helped his nephew. But after a few times, the uncle realized that allowing his nephew to remain unproductive was inappropriate. He decided to teach his nephew a lesson. The next time the nephew approached him, the uncle said, "With determination, even a dead rat can become rich."

Just then, a vagrant passed by. Hearing the uncle's words to his nephew, the vagabond thought to himself, "That makes sense." At that moment, he noticed a dead rat in the courtyard. He picked it up and took it away with him. He washed it up, removed its fur, and cut it into small pieces. After boiling it, he arranged it elegantly and sold it to a fairly wealthy person as cat food.

He used the few coins he earned from this exchange to buy rock sugar. With this rock sugar, he boiled up a sweet drink that he sold for a few more coins, resulting in a slightly greater profit. With that money, he was able to buy a small chick. He raised the chick until it matured into a hen and started laying eggs. Soon he had more little chicks and sold them for even greater profit. Using that money, he went on to buy a goat. In much the same manner, he raised a litter of goats. With his ever-increasing profits, he bought a cow, who soon gave birth to calves. Her milk was also a source of income. This former vagrant was quite industrious. Eventually he opened his own grocery store. Due to his diligent behavior and trustworthiness, his business prospered. He later bought a jewelry store and traded silver and gold, becoming even wealthier.

The man attributed all his current success to the words: "With determination, even a dead rat can become rich." To express his gratitude, he had a golden rat cast and filled its belly with pearls, agate, and gems. He took this treasure and offered it to the uncle of the spoiled child who had spoken that sentence that he overheard. The golden rat represented the sentence that had enabled him to achieve such success. Seeing this, the uncle exclaimed, "this youngster has proven himself worthy of my teaching." He then married his daughter to this young man.

The yellow jambhala's rodent encourages progress and hard work, different from the devotion of Esoteric Buddhism. The moral of this story is that one sentence can influence a person's whole life. Consequently, when relying on Amitābha Buddha's name, it should be remembered that each recitation of "Nā mó ā mí tuó fó" has power. By reciting the Buddha's name, bowing to him, and chanting sutras every day, this accumulated power collects in the mind, filling it with the Pure Land. When we are reborn, it is our strongest impulses that determine which realm we are reborn into. If a practitioner has spent his whole life reciting the Buddha's name, bowing before him, and chanting sutras, this will certainly be the dominant force in the mind. Naturally, such practitioners are reborn into the Pure Land.

Contemplating the Buddha

Most lay Buddhists prefer the practice of reciting the Buddha's name. To fulfill this practice, one must be able to enter the *samādhi* of contemplating the Buddha. The Pure Land Patriarchs originally used meditative concentration during their practice of contemplating the Buddha. The First Patriarch of the Chinese Pure Land School, Huiyuan, advocated meditating upon the Buddha: contemplating the Buddha in the mind, recollecting the Buddha, and visualizing Amitābha Buddha's body rather than the later practice of reciting Amitābha Buddha's name. In the *Contemplation Sutra*, one of the three main Pure Land sutras, contemplation and visualization are the only methods offered. Reciting the Buddha's name is not mentioned. Consequently, monastics usually prefer to train in meditative concentration.

1. The Requirements for Cultivation

The five desires and five hindrances must be completely removed through contemplating the Buddha before one's mind can focus exclusively upon cultivation. Therefore, practitioners' must observe the following in their daily lives:

1. Guard the sense organs: Protect the six sense organs at all times. Do not allow them to drag you into clinging and pursuing external things.

2. Eat and drink in moderation: Know your limits when eating. Do not give rise to greed or aversion.
3. Be dedicated to wakefulness: Even when it is time to sleep, the mind contemplates brightness.
4. Rely upon and abide in right wisdom: After cultivating meditative concentration, one will gradually come to possess this power.

We must remain alert at all times in our everyday lives, watchful of our desire and anger. When external conditions arise, you will quickly see thoughts of greed and anger within the mind. Bring them under control, so that affliction does not arise. This "awareness" of when the mind wanders from a meditation object is called right wisdom. To use a Buddhist term, the discerning quality of this awareness is called *zuoyi* (作意), "gathering attention." Only when the mind can reside within the meditation object can we be said to be meditating with "right mindfulness."

Whatever thoughts arise in the mind, whatever words are spoken, whatever actions are done, all become memories. Memories are impressions left behind by past behaviors. Everyone's *ālaya* consciousness functions both as the seat of memory and as a faculty of discernment. Do you know what to look upon, what not to look upon, what to discuss, what not to discuss, what to do, what not to do, what to listen to, and what not to listen to? It is the *ālaya* consciousness that regulates the mind and knows what is right and wrong, positive and negative, good and evil, difficult and easy.

After we hear the Buddha's teachings, we should "act in accordance with the Dharma," such that our thoughts are in line with the Buddha's teachings. When we come into contact with sense objects we should know: Who is this person? What is going on here? Is this wholesome or unwholesome? It is important to immediately know one's inner thoughts. When sense objects are especially tempting, people who lack meditative concentration are thrown into disarray. Their minds are swept away by sense objects. The goal of meditative concentration is to help us sharpen our reflexes. It helps us to remain alert to what we should and should not look upon, should or should not listen to, should or should not eat, should or should not do, should or should not go.

If we remain alert in our lives, we are able to arrive at the fifth level of mental focus (compliance). This is also called the stage of the "brightened mind" in the Chan School, this is a state in which the mind is consistently bright, pure, clear, and focused. In this state one can uphold the mind in daily life and prevent greed and anger from arising. Otherwise, the mind will fixate itself on every favorable or fascinating sense object that arises and lose itself.

2. The Object of Contemplation

Visualizing the Buddha means creating an image in your mind. Before practicing this kind of contemplation, you should choose a specific image as your meditation object. You can choose any Buddha image with classic iconography. Look into different Buddha images to find the one you favor most. After examining it thoroughly, close your eyes and visualize it in your mind. Take the image as your meditation object. Visual meditation objects are reflections of things we see, and in this sense they are also "images." Each meditation image has different characteristics. For example, the contemplation of impurity is associated with the image of the human body, contemplating the Buddha utilizes an image of the Buddha, and the contemplation of counting the breath uses the images of the nose, *dantian*, or breath. Each of these contemplations are associated with concrete images.

When choosing a meditation object, decide if it will be Śākyamuni Buddha, Amitābha Buddha, or Avalokiteśvara Bodhisattva.

You should not switch between them while training in meditative concentration. If you visualize Amitābha Buddha one moment, Śākyamuni Buddha the next, and Avalokiteśvara Bodhisattva in the end, you will not have sound meditation. If the image you have selected portrays the Buddha or bodhisattva as standing, then visualize them as standing. If the image portrays them as sitting, then visualize them as sitting. Make these kinds of decisions before you begin to practice.

Any Buddha image you choose is likely either a statue or a painting. But when visualizing the Buddha or bodhisattva in your mind, be sure to visualize it's true form. When you perfect your visualization, your image of the Buddha will teach the Dharma to you, shine light on you, and empower you. That is why it is important to treat it as real in your mind. When cultivating meditative concentration, causes will produce corresponding effects. The Buddha image you visualize is a cause, while the manifestation of the Buddha during your visualization is the effect. This is why it is best to visualize the same Buddha image from beginning to end.

3. The Method of Contemplation

When you first start practicing visualization, you can begin with a single feature, such as the eyes of a Buddha image. Suddenly visualizing the entire body of the Buddha with all its details is difficult. This is why the *Contemplation Sutra* suggests beginning by "contemplating the setting sun." In my own humble estimation, this visualization was named after the perfect roundness of Amitābha Buddha's face, similar to the perfect roundness of the sun. As is said in the sutras, "the Buddha's countenance can be likened to a pristine full moon". After one has become accustomed to the visualization of "contemplating the setting sun," imagining an entire face becomes easier. When starting to practice visualization, consider your environment and decide how long you will practice. When your meditation object is really clear and stable, the visualization can be regarded as successful.

When visualizing a Buddha image, you can keep your eyes half closed or fully closed. So long as you can visualize the concrete details of the image, it does not matter if your eyes are slightly open. The image may be clearer this way; everyone's individual habits are different. Some people close their eyes to visualize the Buddha image. Others find the image is easier to visualize if their eyes are slightly opened. See for yourself if having your eyes totally shut suits you, or if having them slightly closed and slightly open works better.

This first hurdle is the most difficult. You will have to spend a lot of time on this first step. If you can visualize the Buddha image's entire silhouette, that is good. If you can't, instead visualize certain traits, like a nose, ears, or eyes. Once you can visualize these traits, focus upon them without stirring.

When beginners visualize the setting sun, the image will grow larger, smaller, float up, sink down, or dissolve away. Afterwards, they will need to try to recreate the image. Overcoming this point is the most difficult, but continue to cultivate with confidence, patience, and perseverance. Of course, one must turn away from the five desires and the five hindrances, and train with confidence and diligence.

When visualizing a Buddha image, once a single feature can be clearly visualized, the rest of the image becomes easier to see. Master Huiyuan's cultivation was so profound that he could close his eyes, clearly visualize Amitābha Buddha, and then open his eyes and the image of Amitābha Buddha remained crystal-clear.

The most crucial point is patience. The faster you attempt to progress on the path, the worse your results will be. If you cultivate quickly, your progress will be slow. If you cultivate slowly, your progress will be quick. The faster you go, the more hurried your mind becomes. Once your mind is hurried, your breathing will become rapid and shallow. With rushed internal energy and a hurried mind, your visualization will wobble and become indistinct. To prevent this, you should relax, take it slow, and serenely cultivate in accordance with causes and conditions. As you become more familiar with this practice, you will progress naturally. You must not become impatient.

If the mind is hurried, your visualized Buddha image will become scattered and lose clarity. That is why it is best to proceed slowly. Even if you can only visualize a single feature of the Buddha image, you will experience great joy. After succeeding at this, you will know that you will definitely be able to successfully visualize the entire body of the Buddha image. After this you can try the second visualization mentioned in the *Contemplation Sutra*: visualizing the water of the Pure Land, as it slowly becomes lapis lazuli.

Through this process of visualization you will learn to see both Amitābha's "direct rewards" of his karma as well as his "indirect rewards." "Direct rewards" refer to the bodies of the Buddhas and bodhisattvas of the Pure Land. "Indirect rewards" refers to the pristine adornments of the Pure Land's mountains, rivers, and bountiful land.

Visualizing Buddha images means creating images in the mind. All forms of meditative concentration use the sixth sense, the mind consciousness, rather than the other five senses. The eye, ear, nose, tongue, and body-consciousnesses function by differentiating phenomena. After passing through the sense organ of our eyes, the adornments of the Buddha will be imprinted in our mind by our sixth consciousness. When sitting in meditation, the sixth consciousness visualizes the Buddha image to train in meditative concentration. This doesn't work by simply placing a Buddha image in front of yourself and staring at it, for the five senses will not lead you to *samādhi*. They are simply used to memorize the appearance of a Buddha image; that is what they are for.

There is a saying in meditation halls, "Take care of your meditation object". This means that after you have created your meditation object, you must constantly care for it and watch it. When you first begin, do not demand that your visualization be perfectly clear, for that would be impossible. You should be pleased to visualize only a silhouette at first. This is quite a rare occurrence. If your practice of contemplating counting the breath is well established, maybe you can briefly glimpse the full glory of Amitābha Buddha's compassionate countenance. If this happens, it is because of your previous training in meditative concentration.

4. "The Mind is the Buddha"

Some practitioners who participate in meditation retreats continue to make reciting the Buddha's name their main practice after they return home. However, after reciting the Buddha's name it is possible to progress to contemplating or visualizing the Buddha. When compared to reciting the Buddha's name, these latter practices are more effective at eradicating karmic obstructions. Furthermore, after you have succeeded at visualization, you can experience the realization that "The mind is the Buddha" and "Buddhahood comes from the mind." Gradually, you can connect with the Chan School.

After you can completely visualize the Buddha image, you will slowly come to a realization: You have not gone to another world, nor has the Buddha come from another world. The image manifested in your mind. The sutras describe this realization as, "Everything is created by the mind. The mind is Buddha and Buddhahood comes from the mind. My mind is precisely Amitābha. Amitābha is precisely my mind. The Pure Land is this very place. This very place is the Pure Land."

Slowly, one will come to think, "Our intrinsic nature and mind are originally pure and clear. This mind is the Buddha. It is because we all have Buddha nature that we are able to become Buddhas." Our confidence in this matter grows with time. The *Flower Adornment Sutra* says, "If people wish to know all the Buddhas of the three time periods, contemplate the nature of the Dharma realm: all things are generated by the mind." I have provided these methods for everyone's reference. Afterwards, readers can try practicing *huatou* training or the contemplation of emptiness.

Contemplating the True Form of the Buddha

Practitioners with great spiritual capacity can practice contemplating the true form of the Buddha to help understand dependent origination.

1. The Three Bodies of All Buddhas

Amitābha Buddha's body is the "direct reward" and the Pure Land is the "indirect reward" that are the results of previous conditions. They did not simply sprout out of nothingness. In a previous life, Amitābha Buddha was born as a king, later becoming a monk named Dharmakara. He vowed to create a sublime Pure Land that would become a land of ultimate bliss. At that time there was a group of princes who shared his wish, Avalokiteśvara Bodhisattva among them, who supported Dharmakara. With their common vow of great compassion, they created a sublime Pure Land wherein they could work together diligently to liberate sentient beings.

Due to Amitābha Buddha's limitless compassion, vows, and his tireless effort to create a Pure Land, his body adapted by becoming unimaginably taller, sublimely adorned, and perfected. His reward body was as vast as Mount Sumeru, which he used to benefit himself and others. Only bodhisattvas who have practiced to the level of the "first ground" will be able to see his reward body. Ordinary beings will only be able to see his manifestation body. The adornments of the Pure Land also rely upon Amitābha Buddha's compassionate vow. That is how the adornments came to exist.

The Pure Land was created through a compassionate vow and for the purpose of liberating sentient beings. Both the direct reward of the Buddha's reward body and the indirect reward of the Pure Land's adornments arise through dependent origination. As the *Diamond Sutra* says, "What is called a large body is not a real large body, and thus it is called a large body."

A Buddha's large body is dependent upon many causes and conditions, and attained through cultivation. It was not always this way. The Buddha's large body is not fixed and unchanging. In simple terms, this is called "the nature of non-self." Because the Buddha's body was not always as large and grand as it now is, the term "large

Three Bodies of the Buddha

The Buddha can be understood as being composed of three aspects, or "bodies." The first is the "manifestation body," which is generated by the Buddha in order to teach and liberate sentient beings. For example, the aspect of Śākyamuni Buddha that walked the earth over 2,500 years ago is the Buddha's manifestation body.

The "reward body" is the supramundane aspect of the Buddha which he has gained through diligent practice. The reward body is able to teach bodhisattvas who are advanced in their practice.

The "Dharma body" is the true form of the Buddha. The Dharma body is eternal and encompasses all of existence. The manifestation body and reward body arise from the Buddha's Dharma body, and later return to the Dharma body.

body" is just a label, even though it has come to its current state through cultivation.

In the same manner, what are called adornments are not adornments, and thus they are called adornments. What is called the world is not the world, but is named the world. The *Diamond Sutra* says that every world is a "unified form" of many causes and conditions. Therefore, they cannot be said to have any self-nature that is self-sufficient, fixed, and unchanging. The body is produced through dependent origination, it does not have self-nature. The Pure Land is also produced through dependent origination, it also does not have self-nature. Whether it is chanting the Buddha's name or contemplating the Buddha, when one succeeds in these practices, one realizes that "the mind is the Buddha" and "Buddhahood comes from the mind." Everything, even Amitābha Buddha's true reward body, arises through dependent origination. Consequently, all these things lack self-nature.

The Elder Subhūti was able to see the Buddha's Dharma body. At the time, the Buddha was already in the Heaven of the Thirty-Three Gods, where he had gone to teach the *Original Vows of Kṣitigarbha Bodhisattva Sutra* to his birth mother. When he returned from heaven, many people came to welcome him back. Only Subhūti remembered the Buddha's words: "To see dependent origination is to see the Dharma. To see the Dharma is to see the Buddha." Only by contemplating dependent origination can one truly see the Buddha. Consequently, Subhūti just sat cross-legged and contemplated dependent origination. As a result, he saw that all phenomena were empty in nature. He then beheld the true totality of the Buddha's Dharma body. Only by observing the Buddha's reward body and transformation body can you see dependent origination. Only then will we be able to enter and contemplate the true form of the Buddha.

2. Contemplation of the Buddha's True Form

Someone who is able to contemplate the true form of the Buddha fully has arrived at the Pure Land. Such a person can see the Buddha's Dharma body. One who knows that nothing comes or goes, and does not arise or cease can fully contemplate the true form of the Buddha. When those with great spiritual capacity possess this kind of wisdom, they will no longer need to travel to the Pure Land and await the "opening of the lotus to see Amitābha Buddha," to awaken to the unborn. They will not need to experience these things, because they have already done so.

If you can see that all phenomena arise due to dependent origination, are born of conditions, and lack an independent intrinsic nature, hold onto this understanding. Let the knowledge that there is no self fill your mind. All phenomena, all worldly things, lack a self. Non-self may seem like a very abstract concept, but you can come to know it through unceasing contemplation of dependent origination, it too is a sort of "image."

We use the images of Buddhas, human bodies, and even corpses during contemplation. Dependent origination, the nature of emptiness, the emptiness of self, and the emptiness of phenomena, are all concepts that come from these images. Therefore it can be said that these images contain the highest spiritual truths. These images are a means to experience the wisdom of enlightenment. If practitioners continue cultivating, they will awaken to the fact that everything within the Dharma realm lacks self-nature. All of them are empty by nature. At this point, one has obtained the wisdom eye and has seen that there is nothing to be seen. This is because all illusory images have been extinguished, leaving one to see the true forms of all phenomena.

3. The Nine Grades of Rebirth

Who is reborn in the Pure Land? First let us consider those with little spiritual capacity: those who do not understand dependent origination and the nature of emptiness. They can enter the Pure Land through their own vow to be reborn there, Amitābha Buddha's compassionate vow to receive them, and wholesome physical, verbal, and mental karma. This is entering the Pure Land through karmic rebirth.

Those of middling spiritual capacity practice contemplating the Buddha, and as such have more powerful meditative concentration. They can produce neutral karma, which is neither wholesome nor unwholesome, but they are not yet enlightened. They will also enter the Pure Land as a karmic rebirth, but will need to continue to practice the thirty-seven aspects of awakening, especially right view and right thought and the three Dharma seals, in order to see the Buddha's Dharma body. This is similar to practitioners who have such great meditative concentration that they can be reborn in the *dhyāna* heavens: though it is a very refined rebirth, they still have a body and are not yet enlightened. As practitioners of middling spiritual capacity practice, they will see that the nature of all phenomena are empty. This is called "the opening of the lotus to see Amitābha Buddha and awakening to the unborn." At this point they have attained enlightenment and have walked the path to its conclusion.

Who then is reborn in the Pure Land? Practitioners of high spiritual capacity can be there now. They don't need to come or go anywhere, and instead be in the Pure Land right here. "Birth and death are *nirvāṇa*. Affliction is *bodhi*." The nature of affliction is empty. Therefore, affliction has no inherent nature unto itself. Birth and death may appear to come and go, but nothing truly comes or goes. This is why birth and death are *nirvāṇa*. This is the wisdom of the highest spiritual capacity: they know they do not need to come or go anywhere.

What about true bodhisattvas, what of them? In all worlds in the ten directions, they liberate living beings. Such true bodhisattvas see the five aggregates as empty. The self, humans, and phenomena; everything is empty. There is nothing that is not empty. The nature of all things is emptiness. There is a Buddhist saying that, "A bodhisattva is like the cool moon wandering through the empty sky." There is no phenomenon that is not empty. Therefore, there are no obstructions.

Everywhere they wander and everywhere they are free. Never do they hesitate to liberate sentient beings. They have no desire for fame or gain. They do not have such narrow hearts as to hoard disciples and temples for themselves. Wherever there are living beings, that is their temple. As long as the world persists, that will be their temple. Because of this, bodhisattvas do not think of a single specific place as the "Pure Land."

These are each different ways to say that all phenomena arise from dependent origination, and therefore lack self-nature. Those with little or middling spiritual capacity do not realize this, and therefore rely on neutral or wholesome karma to guide them to the Pure Land. This is karmic rebirth. Such people have not yet rid themselves of the view of self, and will need to continue to cultivate after arriving in the Pure Land. When the lotus opens and you see Amitābha Buddha and awaken to the unborn, all views of the self are eradicated. Then you have attained the Way.

At first, beginners often have an easier time practicing with a physical Buddha image in front of them. Previously I mentioned that images of emptiness are the "highest spiritual truth." Most ordinary people cannot achieve this. A better approach is to begin the permeating practice of *huatou*. Let me now explain this in detail.

Huatou Training

Training in *huatou*, engaging in doubt—whichever practice you may undertake, you must concentrate and hold onto your *huatou* or the sensation of doubt. Then, in time, delusion and illusory thoughts will be cast aside and you will discover your original face. The principles behind *huatou* training are closely related to cause and effect.

Three Kinds of Karma

One way to analyze karma is into three types: differing karma, similar karma, and increasing karma.

"Differing" karma refers to karma in which the nature of the cause and effect is different. Consider the case of a person who saves the lives of many and is later reborn in a heavenly realm. This is differing karma: the nature of the cause, saving a life, is different from the effect, rebirth in heaven. A similar effect would be having one's life saved in return. Another case of "differing karma" would be someone who harms others and is later reborn in hell. Causes can reach maturation in different ways.

"Similar karma" refers to when habits function as causes that produce effects of the same type. For example, consider someone who has a habit of being greedy. This person's tendency for shamelessness may also grow, as he commits shameful acts to pursue his desires. In this way more habits are produced. Another example: attachment to cleanliness will result in a habit of cleanliness.

"Increasing karma" is when the effect actually strengthens the cause. For example, say you admire the good deeds of others, you may find yourself doing those same good deeds more and more. Wealthy people who make doing good deeds and giving generously a habit will become even wealthier as a result of their wholesome karma. Those who delight in gambling will find their gambling habits increasingly hazardous and intense. Those who delight in drinking alcohol will find themselves drinking more and more.

The actions we do over and over again become habits. *Huatou* training is similar. When we begin, the mind is full of illusory thoughts. After we practice the contemplation of counting the breath and train in *huatou* in the meditation hall we can subdue these illusory thoughts. Slowly, as our practice becomes more and more habitual, illusive thoughts will cease to arise. Our minds become more and more serene.

Just Words Chan

During the Tang Dynasty, there were many enlightened Chan masters in China. These enlightened masters taught their disciples the method to attain enlightenment, and their teachings were passed down as *gongans* (*koans* in Japanese), and then later collected into texts like the *Five Lamp Records*. If practitioners train according to the *gongans* for the purpose of attaining enlightenment, then it does not matter if they meditate in the style of the Chan patriarchs or the Buddha, they will reap great benefit.

Some scholars also enjoy discussing Chan, but they are only playing around with *samādhi* based on words. They may be able to recite the teachings, they lack the least bit of actual skill or training. This is "just words Chan."

One prominent example of this concerns the Song dynasty poet Sū Dōngpō. Once, following momentary fancy, he wrote this poem:

> Bowing, heaven within heaven,
> A light that illuminates the boundless universe,
> The eight winds cannot move me,
> Sitting mindfully upon the purple golden lotus.

Sū Dōngpō then sent someone to deliver his poem to Chan Master Fóyìn.

After the master read the poem, he took up his calligraphy brush and wrote his reply: "Fart!" When he read this, Sū Dōngpō immediately boarded a boat to question Chan Master Fó Yìn. The master laughed heartedly, "You say you are unmoved by the eight winds, and yet a single fart brought you across the river."

People who practice "just words Chan" habitually repeat Chan-sounding phrases over and over until they become like catchphrases. Words that you may utter all the time, whether the occasion is appropriate or not, are like a catchphrase. Such catchphrases and practicing "just words Chan" have no true purpose. However, the fact that repeating words builds habits can be used in Chan cultivation. Allow me to recount a story of one such instance.

Old man Zhang used to like saying "How the heck?" and old man Li liked to say "How on earth?" In time, when old man Zhang's family and friends saw him coming, they did not address him by name, but instead yelled out, "'How the heck' is coming." Old man Li's family and friends started giving him the same treatment, calling out, "'How on earth' is coming."

Both men found the situation quite embarrassing. They made a deal to stop using their catchphrases. Old man Zhang said, "Let's make a bet. From here on, whoever uses their catchphrase again will pay a fine."

Old man Li asked, "How much will the fine be?"

"Whoever slips up first will pay a fine of ten silver ingots."

Old man Li replied, "Very well. From here on in, I won't say it anymore."

After a few days, old man Zhang was looking for someone to chat with and stopped by old man Li's house. He did not see old man Li there, but faintly heard the sound of him moaning and crying out in pain. He asked old man Li's sister-in-law, "Where's old man Li?"

"He's been injured," She said.

"What kind of injury?"

"He broke his foot."

"Ouch! How'd that happen?"

"Yesterday, he went to the outhouse. While he was squatting, a duck stepped on his foot and broke it."

Without so much as a thought, old man Zhang instinctively blurted out, "How the heck?"

Excited, old man Li jumped out from where he had been hiding and exclaimed: "Old man Zhang! I believe you owe ten silver ingots."

Old man Zhang replied, "Darn! You got me." He went on, "I didn't bring any money with me, but I'll pay up sometime soon."

Old man Zhang went back to his home and did not go out for quite a number of days. Old man Li thought to himself, "How on earth could he owe me money like this and not pay up? That's it! I'm going over to his place."

When he arrived at the Zhang residence, he saw old man Zhang's sister-in-law and asked her, "Where's old man Zhang? Is he here?"

She replied, "He went to the police station to file a police report."

"Oh dear! What happened?"

"There was a robbery."

"Was anything taken?"

"Last night some burglars stole the old well from our courtyard."

Old man Li burst out, "How on earth?"

At that moment, old man Zhang appeared saying, "We're even now. We don't owe each other any money."

3. Choosing a Huatou

After training in a certain *huatou* for a while, the words will become a sort of catchphrase. Day after day, you will think, "Who is reciting the Buddha's name? Who is reciting the Buddha's name?"

Or when reciting Amitābha Buddha's name, you might experience sensations of doubt, thinking, "Who is reciting the Buddha's name?" These types of habitual questions can help to focus the mind. Counting the breath, sensations of doubt, and training in *huatou* are all useful methods for cultivation. Once they become habits, deluded and illusory thoughts will no longer arise.

If you want to remove some of your afflictions or learn to let go more easily, there are plenty of lines from the *Heart Sutra* and the *Diamond Sutra* that can be adopted as a *huatou*. For example, if something is causing you anger, think to yourself, "All forms are illusory." If you really want something that you cannot have, think, "'All conditioned phenomena are like dreams, illusions, bubbles, and shadows'... they are not real!" You might then consider, "Hmmm... It really is just like a dream, illusion, bubble, or shadow. Even if I did get this, it would just conditionally exist for a few decades." In this way the mind will be relieved.

These are just bits of wisdom that come from understanding the nature of emptiness. They can help to cure a scattered mind, but they are not the same as the true, supreme wisdom that comes from entering *samādhi*. However, they can still help to remove afflictions and subdue habits.

What is Brightening the Mind?

Whether through *huatou* training or contemplating a meditation object, eventually you will arrive at the stage of the "brightened mind," in which practitioners have an excellent understanding of their own mental processes. It is worth mentioning that some meditation objects make it a bit more difficult to remove affliction and realize the nature of emptiness. For example, contemplating water, earth, or space all have their merits, as do the contemplation of blue, yellow, red, or bright light, but these visual contemplations are not

particularly strong or powerful when it comes to eliminating affliction and subduing habits.

No matter what meditation object you use, what matters is
whether or not you are able to diligently and single-mindedly abide
within the meditation object. After you spend enough time practicing, you will certainly develop single-minded focus and attain the
state of the "brightened mind." Through reciting the Buddha's name,
one can enter the *samādhi* of contemplating the Buddha. Likewise,
a person engaged in *huatou* training can focus on a phrase so completely that illusory thoughts cease. Gradually the mind develops
and becomes pure.

Enter *samādhi* and the body and mind relax. This helps to subdue habits. Where once you may have been impulsive, with a bright
mind you will be focused and in control when facing external phenomena. You can know what is wholesome or unwholesome, and
what thoughts are pure or impure. You will be able to properly manage physical, verbal, and mental behavior. There are some Chan
practitioners who think just this state is enlightenment. Actually,
this is just using meditative concentration to subdue habits. This is
what life is like when the mind is bright.

Whether it is *huatou* training, focusing upon a meditation object, or
engaging in doubt, all of these practices develop the same skills. Within
a meditation hall, each person should follow their own interests. If this
means *huatou* training or the sensation of doubt, both are fine. I hope
that everyone can use the wisdom of emptiness or accept the three
Dharma seals. Train so that your own scattered mind contains thoughts
of "impermanence" or "non-self" within daily life. One will gradually
develop the powers of penetrating vision and the ability to let go.

I encourage everyone to take either "All forms are illusory," or
"All conditioned phenomena are like dreams, illusions, bubbles, and
shadows" as a *huatou*. Let these phrases become your catchphrases,

appearing in your mouth at all times. "All forms are illusory," after you have contemplated this saying long enough, and your mind is focused upon it, then you will remember it whenever you encounter any sense object. Though you may not yet have direct knowledge of the nature of emptiness, you may understand emptiness and dependent origination as concepts. With the additional tools of your *huatou*, you will be prepared to deal with whatever afflictions appear before you. Your power of concentration will deepen, your wisdom will increase, and eventually, you will able to understand the empty and serene nature of dependent origination.

Chapter Six

BODHI MIND

Buddhism concerns itself with questions about life. Why do people suffer? What is the cause of suffering? What can be done to remove suffering so people can experience happiness? In total, the Buddha's teachings are comprised of questions about human existence and how to lead a perfect life.

Humanistic Buddhism

The term "Humanistic Buddhism" can be interpreted in two ways. One is to see it as an elucidation of the bodhisattva path as discussed in Mahāyāna Buddhism. This includes the teachings on the six perfections and the four means of embracing, both of which consider interpersonal relationships, and how to treat others with mutual respect and understanding. They also discuss how people can share their happiness and be mutually beneficial to one another. If we could all help one another in this way, we could create a world of infinite virtue. This is one way of understanding Humanistic Buddhism.

The term "Humanistic Buddhism" also refers to the fact that we can only practice the Buddha's teachings and become Buddhas while living in the human realm, because human beings have the ability

Four Means of Embracing

The four means of embracing are methods through which bodhisattvas ingratiate themselves to and liberate sentient beings. They four means are:

• Giving material things, fearlessness, and the Dharma as needed by sentient beings, so that they are free from worry and despair.

• Kind words that praise and encourage sentient beings to increase their faith.

• Empathy when helping others, so that we understand the plight of sentient beings, and can help them through their problems together, so that they faithfully accept the teachings.

• Altruism that attends to the needs of sentient beings so that they can be introduced to the wisdom of the Buddhas.

to control themselves. Beings are reborn in the human realm, heavenly realm, *asura* realm, hell realm, hungry ghost realm, or animal realm. To attain the highest virtues, people must overcome all sorts of obstacles. People can perfect their character through the purity of their practices and the purity of their minds.

Unlike other sentient beings, humans have a sense of moral shame, which can be a powerful force for people to better themselves. Humans can differentiate between right and wrong. After examining the interplay of good and evil through the lens of history, humans seek to improve the bad, sustain the good, and continue on the path of progress.

The human realm contains both suffering and happiness, and those who experience both learn to distance themselves from one and seek the other. It becomes a goal: avoid suffering, attain happiness. These conditions make the human realm a more advantageous rebirth than even rebirth in a heavenly realm. The saying that "man can conquer the heavens" supports the idea that only those born in the human realm can succeed on the Buddhist path. This is the most important aspect of Humanistic Buddhism. As human beings, the most difficult qualities to develop are right contemplation, discernment, restraint, and strong resolve. If we understand Humanistic Buddhism in this way, then we will treasure our human bodies.

The Wish for Enlightenment

Those who clearly understand the Buddha's teachings will inevitably vow to liberate all sentient beings. I hope that everyone can give rise to what we call the "*bodhi* mind:" the intention to attain enlightenment for the benefit of all sentient beings. Śākyamuni Buddha too cultivated the bodhisattva path through many lifetimes and worked to liberate all sentient beings.

The iconic physical appearance of the Buddha is described by the "thirty-two marks of excellence" and "eighty notable characteristics." These physical attributes are simply all the merit and virtues that the Buddha attained through many lifetimes of wholesome deeds. Just as the specifics of a person's good deeds differ, so too do their appearances. To cultivate merit and wisdom, one must follow the bodhisattva path. Only then will our efforts lead to infinite merit and virtue.

Among Chinese Buddhists, some single-mindedly pursue rebirth in Amitābha Buddha's Western Pure Land. Others endeavor to brighten the mind and see their nature so they can quickly become Buddhas. This is the goal of meditation. The goal of observing emptiness is to realize the true nature of phenomena. The goal of reciting Amitabha Buddha's name is rebirth in his Pure Land. All of these are excellent practices, but it is essential that all practitioners give rise to the *bodhi* mind. Such people vow to liberate all sentient beings over the course of many lifetimes, and renew this vow every day. In this way one applies the spirit of Mahāyāna.

Some people are not brave enough to make a vow that requires such a long-term commitment. That said, liberation from the cycle of birth and death is not the same as leaving the world behind. To be liberated from the cycle of birth and death means understanding that the natures of birth and death are inherently tranquil.

There is a Buddhist saying, "Birth and death are *nirvāṇa*. Affliction is *bodhi*." All afflictions lack self-nature. How do afflictions arise? Because the six sense organs contact the six sense objects and give rise to discrimination, comparison, and attachment, suffering arises.

Affliction is produced through dependent origination. It does not produce itself. Even thoughts are produced through dependent origination. They too are empty by nature. Therefore, they share the same substance as enlightenment. Birth and death are illusory. Sentient beings are not born and do not die. They neither come nor go. What comes and goes are illusory images subject to creation and destruction, they lack any sort of true essence. That is why it is said "Birth and death are *nirvāṇa*."

Unwholesome karma does not simply go away after we've attained enlightenment and are liberated from birth and death. That is simply not possible! Even after liberating yourself from birth and death, all the unwholesome karma produced in the past stays with you. So how can we be liberated from birth and death? Liberation can be attained by understanding that ignorance is illusory and thereby putting an end to generating new karma.

Since the distant past, beings have taken the many things of this world to be real. Because of this, people discriminate, and give rise to greed and attachment, creating powerful compulsions of desire. The force of these desires cause us to act and form habits. Once people understand that the nature of ignorance is empty and all things are illusory, they will put aside their desires and delusions for the things of this world. Then the pull of worldly things will cease.

Our old karma stays with us. But after we rid ourselves of our attachment to the self, such karma loses its pull and momentum. Such conditions limit the force of past karma to bear fruit. It is like a rice paddy that is stripped of water and mud: it no longer has the proper conditions for the seedlings to sprout.

Liberation does not mean casting aside all the karma one has ever created. Karma cannot be discarded. Liberation means stopping the perpetuation of karma by abandoning false views, such as greed and attachment. When the forces that propel the cycle of karma end, one can be liberated.

Sentient beings need our care. They need us to give rise to the *bodhi* mind. After enlightenment you can control the arising of the mind and its thoughts. One can realize the truth of the *Heart Sutra*, that there is "No eye, ear, nose, tongue, body, or mind," and "No form, sound, smell, taste, touch or *dharmas*." We come to view all sense objects as empty and insubstantial. This allows us to extinguish our habits caused by greed, anger, and delusion so that we may liberate all sentient beings. This allows us to perfect our merit and wisdom. During this process, we must give rise to the *bodhi* mind, if we hope to realize supreme enlightenment.

Dependent Origination and the Bodhi Mind

If you think about dependent origination over the vast expanse of time, you can see that all people have parents who, in turn, have parents of their own. Follow this logic back one thousand or two thousand years, multiplying in this manner, and it becomes hard to imagine how many beings are part of your family. The number of relationships we share with other beings in this life is innumerable.

Imagine how many more relationships we have over the course of our many lives.

At present, everyone has a "self" that experiences extreme happiness or anger from time to time. Sometimes causes and conditions lead people to do great things. Sometimes causes and conditions lead people to do terrible things. There are even some people who, due to the depth of their merit and virtue, appear to not produce any negative karma. However, this does not mean that their mind is untainted by anger.

All sentient beings have greed, anger, and delusion. As such, the parents, siblings, and relatives we've had over our many lives all have potential for both great good and great evil. To use an example from modern society, there are cases wherein siblings take each other to court in order to fight over an inheritance, refusing to hold the funeral until the matter is settled. This is an example of family turning into enemies.

As we continue on from lifetime to lifetime, those who were our loved ones in previous lives may no longer be our loved ones in this life. Maybe the people whom we detested in previous lives now surround us. All of the people who we detest now were once people we loved in a previous life. Both love and hate take shape according to cause and effect. Those whose actions are mutually beneficial become friends, and those whose actions are in conflict with one another become enemies. It has always been this way.

Countries are the same. The relationship between Mainland China and Taiwan shows how people can go from being family to enemies. Once a relationship of mutual benefit is restored, the two countries will go from being enemies to being family once again. Don't all human interactions unfold like this? Doesn't it then become hard to tell love from hate? Power, status, wealth, emotions, and other such things are the external causes and conditions which produce love and hate.

When we consider all of our relatives from previous lives, some have inevitably been reborn in the heavenly realms, some in the human realm, and some are reborn in the realms of hell, hungry ghosts, and animals. According to dependent origination, all sentient beings are our parents, siblings, and relatives from previous lives. Having acquired this wisdom through their observations on dependent origination, bodhisattvas are unwilling to abandon even a single sentient being.

Of course, some sentient beings are stubborn and resistant. When bodhisattvas encounter such people, they feel great sympathy, and wait until the causes and conditions are right to help them, but nonetheless would never give up on such beings. Take for example the Indian Queen Śrīmālā, who never abandoned any sentient beings. As long as bodhisattvas have sufficient conditions, words, or power, they will liberate any being, embracing them. By observing dependent origination with wisdom, bodhisattvas are thereby able to give rise to hearts of great, unconditional loving-kindness and compassion.

As all sentient beings are products of the combination of the five aggregates, their nature is empty. We are empty. Others are empty. Although every entity in the world has differences and unique attributes, they all share the same nature: emptiness, without differences or qualities. Thus it is said, "All phenomena are equal. There is no superior or inferior."

All phenomena are empty of distinctions or boundaries, and as such their nature is empty. The essence of phenomena does not arise or cease. In a way, all phenomena have their own individual qualities which are somewhat unique. They are the same as the light cast from a cluster of lamps. The light emanating from each individual lamp is somewhat unique. However, once the lights have been cast outward, they intermix until no boundaries or gaps exist between them. The lamps join together.

In the same regard, in emptiness, all sentient beings are one. By looking into the emptiness of dependent origination, we can see that all sentient beings are of the same essence. For this reason, bodhisattvas see themselves as the same as all sentient beings. In this world, sentient beings experience attachment, defilement, and clinging. They are surrounded by obstacles and suffering. Because we are all one, until all sentient beings are liberated, a bodhisattva will not be satisfied.

Only by giving rise to a heart of great compassion and liberating all sentient beings can bodhisattvas become Buddhas. Therefore, the heart of great compassion that bodhisattvas possess means completing oneself by completing others. According to dependent origination, all sentient beings are each connected with all others. But from the perspective of emptiness, all sentient beings can be seen as equal in essence. This is why bodhisattvas give rise to the *bodhi* mind, and generate hearts of great, unconditional loving-kindness and compassion. Only through seeing the emptiness of dependent origination can one attain enlightenment. Only then can one act with a heart of great, unconditional loving-kindness and compassion.

Chapter Seven

TYPES OF WISDOM

Do we practice for the cultivation of merit? Do we practice for the cultivation of meditative concentration? Do we practice for the cultivation of wisdom? There are many Buddhist practitioners who cultivate merit and meditative concentration, but few who can be said to cultivate wisdom.

You may think, "I talk about the sutras and read contemporary books on Buddhism. How can you say I do not cultivate wisdom?" The cultivation of wisdom requires unceasing contemplation. Only then can it be considered cultivating wisdom. Giving a talk on the Dharma, expounding Buddhist sutras, and forging wholesome affinities cannot alone be considered the cultivation of wisdom. One must have right view.

Developing right view requires unceasing wise contemplation. The "right thought" path factor within the Noble Eightfold Path can also be included among the three qualities of *prajñā*. In this instance, "right thought" corresponds to "*prajñā* of contemplation." It is quite rare to be able to apply wisdom throughout one's life, even among monastics. Consequently, the number of people who are free from the cycle of birth and death are few.

Three Qualities of Prajñā

Prajñā is the Sanskrit word for wisdom. In a Buddhist context, prajñā refers to wisdom which surpasses worldly knowledge. This kind of wisdom has three special qualities:

1. Prajñā of true reality, which is a profound understanding of the nature of reality

2. Prajñā of contemplation, which is the ability to see the true nature of reality in all phenomena.

3. Prajñā of skillful means, which is the ability to skillfully discern the differing characteristics of phenomena for the purpose of teaching the Dharma.

Differences between
Meditative Concentration and Wisdom

If you wish to become an *arhat* and attain liberation from birth and death, you should first start with correcting your own thinking. This is cultivating "right thought" according to the Noble Eightfold Path, which is the same as "right mindfulness." The four bases of mindfulness encompass the "right mindfulness" path factor, and are of extreme importance. "Right mindfulness" is another aspect of meditative concentration. It means to be mindful of the phenomena of the world, and observant of their nature. It is complementary to right thought. Together, right mindfulness and right thought can liberate us from birth and death. The *prajñā* of contemplation is to see all things in accordance with the Middle Way, and see that all things are empty.

Form and emptiness are the same. Form arises through dependent origination, but the law of dependent origination is itself empty. Form is an illusion; it is temporary and subject to change. Its nature is inherently empty. To speak of emptiness in terms of the material and to understand and observe emptiness within the material is true wisdom.

No matter how much one talks about *prajñā* and the twelve links of dependent origination, unless one can develop the *prajñā* of contemplation in life, such talk is merely admiring another's treasures. The concepts belong to someone else. In Chinese Buddhist practice there is the Esoteric School in which one practices by reciting mantras thousands upon thousands of times. This is certain to eliminate karmic obstructions and increase blessings.

Only after completing preliminary practices, such as cultivating meditative concentration and stopping and seeing meditation can you enter the gates of wisdom. If all one does is cultivate merit and virtue, then practicing meditative concentration will not be easy. A mind that is rushed, desperate for volume and accomplishment, and is determined to complete the practice as soon as possible is not in line with the Middle Way.

Settling the mind by reciting the Buddha's name to enter *samādhi* is another way to practice meditative concentration. This method removes karmic obstructions and increases merit, such that it is both cultivating merit and meditative concentration. The Chan School focuses more on the cultivation of meditative concentration than the cultivation of wisdom. Some people have a difficult time accepting this. Some believe that by training in *huatou* and confronting doubt that they are cultivating wisdom. However, those who train in *huatou* merely observe their intentions and study the condition of the mind before recalling the *huatou*. After questioning, they contemplate, "Who is thinking right now? Who is that?" This kind of contemplation is not the same as contemplating dependent origination or emptiness.

Different methods will have different results. Once meditative concentration has brightened the mind, illusory thoughts will cease and the mind will become pure, pristine, and crystal-clear. Negative karma will cease. Whether you are walking, standing, sitting, or lying down, you will remain composed, light, and blissful. The power of one's meditative concentration can prevent deluded thoughts from arising. Because of this, people often confuse "meditative concentration" with "wisdom," thinking that they have become sages, when they have only developed meditative concentration.

The Buddha said we should see the five aggregates as empty. As it says in the *Diamond Sutra*, "all conditioned phenomena are like dreams, illusions, bubbles, and shadows." "Seeing" in this way is how we uphold wisdom. Deep observation is how we practice wisdom. Meditative concentration is focusing the mind at a single point. When the mind abides in this one point, wisdom arises through discernment and examination.

Three Steps to Develop Wisdom

One way to understand wisdom is by analyzing the methods of acquiring wisdom. In this way, the development of wisdom can be broken down into three steps:

1. Wisdom from hearing arises from listening to the Buddhist teachings and reading Buddhist writings. This kind of wisdom develops one's faith and understanding of the Dharma.

2. Wisdom from thinking is the contemplation of the Buddhist teachings and how they apply to the causes and conditions of life itself.

3. Wisdom from practice combines the above with cultivating meditative concentration. This generates wisdom that is not only grounded in deep understanding, but in direct knowledge and experience.

Now that you understand the definition of wisdom and meditative concentration, ask yourself: "Does my practice emphasize meditative concentration or wisdom?" Compare the two and find out.

Wisdom from Hearing

Those who wish to study Buddhism and attain enlightenment do so through thinking. It is impossible for those beginning to learn Buddhism not to think in terms of wholesome and unwholesome. They do not yet have the ability to do so. They must first awaken to the true forms of the world, human existence, and the universe. Listen to these truths deeply and one is said to develop "wisdom from hearing." However, this kind of "hearing" is not passive, but requires reflecting and examining things for yourself.

When Śāriputra heard that "All phenomena arise from causes and conditions, and they cease by causes and conditions," why was he so taken aback? He reflected upon this matter himself, comparing this teaching to his everyday observations of the universe and human existence before acknowledging that the Buddha's theory was correct. That is why he was elated. He brought his friend the honorable Maudgalyāyana to go and together become disciples of the Buddha.

After hearing the Buddha's teachings, you should process and reflect upon them. The teaching that "all phenomena arise from causes and conditions, and they cease by causes and conditions," should not be acquired solely through meditative concentration, but thoroughly understood. This is wisdom. You can spend whole days repeatedly chanting the *Diamond Sutra* or the *Heart Sutra* and it will be of no use, because such supreme wisdom is being treated as just a way to gain merit.

Of course, allowing teachings from the sutras like "The perfection of wisdom is not the perfection of wisdom, and that that is what is called the perfection of wisdom," "Adornment is not adornment, and that that is what is called adornment," and "Sentient beings are not sentient beings, and that that is what is called sentient beings," to permeate throughout your life will benefit this life and future lives.

However, if we read the sutras without reflecting upon their doctrine there will be a lot of confusion. Why does the *Diamond Sutra* say "there is no notion of self, notion of others, notion of sentient beings, or notion of longevity"? How can you uphold the six perfections "without abiding in anything" as the *Diamond Sutra* teaches? What does it mean to live "without abiding in anything"? How should we abide?

How many people really understand the phrase, "realized the five aggregates are empty" from the *Heart Sutra*? When people chant the sutras, they usually do so to eliminate karmic obstructions and accumulate merit. Few are trying to develop wisdom, and therefore it is not easy for them to attain enlightenment and liberation. Though they read the sutras often, they do not turn all that they hear into wisdom.

We speak often of morality, meditative concentration, and wisdom. In Mahāyāna Buddhism, aside from upholding precepts and cultivating meditation, one also develops wisdom, called *prajñā*. Morality, meditative concentration, and wisdom are also three of the six perfections. The factors of the Noble Eightfold Path can also be classified according to morality, meditative concentration, and wisdom. The Buddha taught that to develop wisdom we must listen, reflect, and practice. Within Chinese Buddhism we could be said to be good at "listening," but we lack complete understanding. As such, though we have listened to much and have great intellect, most cannot be said to have "right view."

"Right view" comes from examining dependent origination. Only by contemplating the universal law of cause and effect one step at a time can one arrive upon "right view". Through examination one can see that all arising and cessation is conditioned and dependent. Therefore, all mental formations are impermanent, compounded, and lacking self-nature. When all phenomena are seen as illusory and arising from causes and conditions, you can understand the *Heart Sutra* when it says all phenomena "neither arise nor cease."

This is why we need the three Dharma seals. For Buddhists, "the three Dharma seals" are used to determine if a theory is in accord with the Buddha's teaching. Though we may not yet see the wisdom and reasoning behind the three Dharma seals, by constantly observing the workings of the universal law of karma we can gradually come to have right view. When right view is paired with wisdom, the result is the three Dharma seals.

The three Dharma seals can be used in your daily life. When you encounter an unpleasant sense object, use the three Dharma seals by applying "right view." Remember, "All conditioned phenomena are impermanent," so let things be, and let go. Remember, "All phenomena are without self-nature," let things be and see through them. If something lacks self-nature, what is there to desire? By turning all you hear into wisdom, you gain this kind of confident resolve. This is how you know you have accomplished the difficult task of turning all you hear into wisdom.

Wisdom from Thinking

Without complete understanding of the Buddha's teachings, you cannot hope to transform your thinking into wisdom. Turning your thinking into wisdom is the "right thought" factor of the Noble Eightfold Path. This sort of thinking is the unceasing contemplation of impermanence and non-self in all things, exemplified by the words of the *Diamond Sutra:* "All conditioned phenomena are like dreams, illusions, bubbles, and shadows." This is transforming your thinking into wisdom.

Think of sourness and saliva will build up in your mouth. Think of what you desire and the endocrine system will create various changes. Only by developing right thought can you remedy negative dispositions like greed, anger, jealousy, and resentment. Only the constant thought that "all things are illusory" can you develop the means to subdue impulses and actions. To completely subdue affliction we must think in accordance with the Dharma, practice right thought, and develop the *prajñā* of contemplation.

"Desire" is what happens after we encounter a sense object and we have a pleasant feeling. We come to constantly reminiscence, remember, and think about these sense objects, inducing various physical and verbal behaviors. The contemplation of impurity uses this same process to remove desire by giving rise to unpleasant feelings. When we contemplate how corpses start to smell, then rot, then become worm-infested, ending up as nothing more than pale bones, this naturally gives rise to aversion and suppresses desire.

Removing affliction can't be achieved with just an ordinary level of meditative concentration. Meditation can lessen affliction, but to completely sever it, meditative concentration must be combined with the development of wisdom. Eliminating affliction in this way allows us to uphold morality—how else could we realize morality, meditative concentration, and wisdom together?

"Ignorance" is a mental problem. Wisdom is needed to think properly, and right view is necessary to eliminate ignorance. In addition to meditative concentration and morality, wisdom has the force to permanently remove our habits. Developing wisdom from thinking is to reflect constantly and properly, like those arhats who liberated themselves. They see all within the world as impermanent, and are thus able to truly leave the world behind.

Developing wisdom from thinking is a matter of subduing and removing affliction. This is the same as the *prajñā* of contemplation.

Through right thought upon the three Dharma seals you can be liberated from birth and death, attain awakening, and become an *arhat.*

Wisdom from Practice

To develop wisdom from practice, your meditative concentration and wisdom must have already reached a certain level. Specifically, you must be able to enter *samādhi.* One must constantly reflect upon the words from the *Heart Sutra,* "form is not different from emptiness, emptiness is not different from form." All that arises through dependent origination has the nature of emptiness. Since all phenomena are empty, many conditions must come together for them to arise.

Reflect on this. Cultivate meditative concentration unceasingly. If you have not yet entered *samādhi,* such reflections are merely wisdom from a scattered mind. Such wisdom can still subdue affliction, but it is not the kind of wisdom which leads to being completely without outflows.

As mentioned earlier, all phenomena arise from a combination of causes and conditions, and therefore lack self-nature. It is important to note that the Buddhist use of the term "self" is rather specific, and refers to the ability to exist independently of other phenomena, never change, be self-perpetuating, and self-sufficient. In Buddhism, "non-self" doesn't mean that we shouldn't use the word "I" or "me" to distinguish an individual from others.

The nature of non-self is tranquility. What is tranquility? It is difficult for a scattered mind to be tranquil, and as such this concept is not easily understood. The best way to understand tranquility is to cultivate the four bases of mindfulness, contemplate the three Dharma seals, and examine all phenomena as empty and without self-nature. In this way you will slowly enter *samādhi,* and upon exiting this focused meditation state wisdom without outflows will arise. This is tranquility.

This kind of wisdom arises after entering *samādhi*. This state is without outflows, and one sees that all phenomena are created through conditions and lack an inherent nature. This is a state of non-discrimination, which can be known through non-discriminating wisdom.

Non-discriminating wisdom will see a non-discriminated world. When you enter *samādhi*, all of your thoughts "do not arise or extinguish, are not defiled or pure, and do not increase or decrease," for one sees that all things are illusory. Cultivating in this way joins the *prajñā* of contemplation with the *prajñā* of true reality. This is the culmination of developing wisdom from practice.

In the course of studying Buddhism you will need to learn how the Noble Eightfold Path, the twelve links of dependent origination, the *Heart Sutra*, the *Diamond Sutra,* and the Mahāyāna sutras and commentaries are all interlinked together. Afterwards, you should not neglect the Noble Eightfold Path, for it is the only way to be liberated from birth and death. The six perfections of the bodhisattva path are the only way to become a Buddha. The two cannot be separated.

Only the Noble Eightfold Path can allow us to see the five aggregates as empty, know that there is no notion of self or other, and practice the bodhisattva path. After mastering the Buddha's teachings, you will know how to act skillfully in everyday life. What parts of our practice are cultivating wisdom, and which are cultivating merit? What is developing meditative concentration, and what is developing wisdom? We should understand these matters so that we do not waste the precious seconds of our lives.

Chapter Eight

REALIZATION

A nyone who learns the Buddha's teachings will want to attain enlightenment sooner rather than later, and will enter the meditation hall intent on brightening the mind and seeing their true nature. This is all well and good, but it is important to understand that our habits cannot be removed and purified within a single meditation retreat. The process continues even *after* attaining an initial realization.

Within the meditation hall you may engage in seated meditation, *huatou* training, or other such practices. When engaged in such practice you may have a breakthrough and come to understand the truth of phenomena. This is a meditative realization: to put it simply, knowing the truth of the universe and human existence.

What is Realization?

Before the great disciple Śāriputra met Śākyamuni Buddha, he and Maudgalyāyana were both established leaders in religious traditions of the time. Both believed that their understanding of the universe and human existence was unsurpassed. But when Aśvajit Bhikṣu, one of the Buddha's first five disciples, shared with them the words, "all phenomena arise from causes and conditions, and they cease from causes and conditions," Śāriputra was struck with a sudden realization. He realized that everything within the world is born of causes and conditions and through causes and conditions they are extinguished. This is the great truth of Buddhism.

Many Buddhists want to explore the teachings within the great Buddhist sutras and treatises, and hope to pour over the entire Buddhist canon, reading and re-reading its texts. While this is good, a wise individual, like Śāriputra, can have a realization from hearing just a single phrase. When such a thing happens it is certainly wonderful. But reading through all twelve divisions of the Buddhist canon simply means that one is well-read. Without developing right view based on dependent origination, then all that reading is meaningless.

There is a Buddhist verse that says, "If a person lives to be one hundred but does not see the teaching of arising and ceasing, they are lesser than one who has lived a single day but has understood the teaching." What is life? What is death? This is the teaching of dependent origination. If you fully understand this teaching, you are a "great hearer of the Dharma." To understand dependent origination, understand the wisdom of emptiness. To experience dependent origination, experience the wisdom of emptiness. Cultivate in this way and you will have a realization. Then you will truly be a "great hearer of the Dharma."

Dependent origination shows how all worldly phenomena are illusory, but we should take this understanding one step further. The Buddha's teaching of dependent origination also shows how the nature of all phenomena is equal and tranquil. Enlightenment confirms the tranquil nature of all things. After you understand the true form of all phenomena and find your own original face you will truly know dependent origination.

When he heard that "all phenomena arise from causes and conditions, and they cease from causes and conditions," Śāriputra had a realization then and there. He came to know that nothing within the world is independently created, independently existent, or independently complete. He saw that all things are illusory. However, from within these illusions, what is true and real can be found. Knowing true reality is the ability to see illusory phenomena, know that they are not real, and know that they arise and cease dependent on conditions. This is how you can attain realization.

Cultivation after Realization

When learning Buddhism, especially Humanistic Buddhism, we continue to develop and practice even after attaining initial realization. It is important to approach Buddhism with this kind of attitude. When it comes to realization, there is a Buddhist saying that one with little doubts will have little realization, one with great doubts will have great realization, and one with no doubts will have no realization. This is the kind of realization that comes from training in *huatou* and engaging in doubt.

How we practice after initial realization is grounded in first knowing dependent origination. Seeing the true form of worldly phenomena can change our perspective on the world, and guide our practice. When we know that all things arise through causes and conditions and are illusory, we can abandon attachment and defilement. From then on we continue the gradual process of cultivation.

All of us have long taken the things of the world to be real, and this has resulted in many forms of attachment and defilement, including clinging to views. We should uphold the precepts so that we can be in control of ourselves. So much of our behavior, from the way we talk, the "catchphrases" we may use, and our mannerisms are all habits we form.

How do these habits come to be? They are the result of past ig-norance, for a time when we did not know the truth of worldly phenomena. At that time, we continually pursued all the forms of enjoyment to be had within the world. Those pursuits became our habits. Now that we more fully understand them, we can control these impulses by upholding the precepts, so that we can avoid harming others.

We can apply the Noble Eightfold Path in our daily lives by practicing right speech through speaking in accordance with the Dharma, right action by living righteously, and right livelihood by maintaining a reasonable household.

Practitioners should control themselves in their daily lives. They should respect others and not harm them. Though our actions can be suppressed, our habits are powerful and difficult to subdue. Even if actions, movements, and expressions could be forcibly controlled, we cannot let go of the thoughts in the mind. When faced with pleas-ant sense objects, the mind always gives rise to deluded thoughts, discrimination, and irrationality. That is why it is necessary to culti-vate meditative concentration and give rise to right mindfulness and right meditative concentration.

Cultivating Right Mindfulness and Right Meditative Concentration

What is right mindfulness? Right mindfulness means that your thoughts accord with right view, right thought, and the wisdom of emptiness. It also means focusing on a meditation object that re-duce affliction and leads to the truth. Contemplating the body as impure, contemplating feelings as suffering, contemplating the mind as impermanent, and contemplating phenomena as non-self are four meditation objects classified as "right mindfulness." They reduce af-fliction and lead to the truth.

It is important to note that a "meditation object" in this sense means what you focus your intention, contemplation, and concentration on. However, you can actually contemplate a "meditation object" for the successful development of either meditative concentration or wisdom.

The three Dharma seals are one such meditation object: "All conditioned phenomena are impermanent," "all phenomena are without self-nature," and "*nirvāṇa* is perfect tranquility." Contemplating these abides by the Middle Way and dependent origination, and is thus "right mindfulness."

What is right meditative concentration? You can let go of worldly power and the five desires gradually through regular, daily practice of right mindfulness. When you then enter *samādhi*, or are on the cusp of doing so, you are unlikely to give rise to unwholesome habits, as you already accord with the Middle Way. This is right meditative concentration.

In everyday life, one's personality should be gentle and one's thoughts free of delusion. One should be without desire, defilement, or attachment to views, so that one will accord with the Way. From contemplating impermanence, non-self, impurity, suffering, and other such concepts, one can enter *samādhi*. The attainment of *samādhi* is indicative of the mind of renunciation. The mind of renunciation is *samādhi* without outflows. It is pure, pristine, in accordance with the Middle Way, and in line with the teaching of emptiness. Entering *dhyāna* is right meditative concentration.

Right mindfulness, made up of the four bases and mindfulness and the three Dharma seals, allows you to give rise to the mind of renunciation and wisdom without outflows. When this is combined with right meditative concentration and right view, one can enter the truth, enter emptiness, and be liberated from birth and death.

When learning Buddhism, you must have right view and right thought. Only then can you know the wisdom of emptiness and see the five aggregates as empty. In this way you can experience realization, confirm realization, and unlock realization. Afterwards, you will contemplate impermanence, non-self, and the other bases of mindfulness regularly. You will become dispassionate, unattached, and able to see through worldly illusion. This is liberation in this very life.

Contemplating Non-Self

In the *Diamond Sutra*, Śākyamuni Buddha clearly describes the contemplation of great bodhisattvas. The content of the *Diamond Sutra* was spoken for Mahāyāna bodhisattvas. People shouldn't associate doctrines like impermanence and non-self only with arhats. That would be greatly mistaken. There are no Buddhas or bodhisattvas who have not contemplated non-self. As mentioned in the *Heart Sutra*, before he was liberated, Avalokiteśvara Bodhisattva contemplated the emptiness of the self, and saw that the five aggregates were empty.

In the *Diamond Sutra*, "the contemplation of non-self" is the concept discussed by the highest-ranking bodhisattvas. With the view of non-self, and no notion of self and no notion of others, bodhisattvas proceed to practice all good deeds. After setting aside the self, these good deeds do not abide in form, sound, smell, taste, touch, or *dharmas,* and are thus in line with *bodhi. Bodhi* means enlightenment, and has the nature of emptiness. Such bodhisattvas are removed from notions of self and other and perform all good deeds. They can see the empty nature of those who give, those who receive, and the gift itself and practice the six perfections. In this way they acquire merit without the nature of merit.

Living in accord with emptiness in this way is the foundation for becoming a Buddha. If your sense of ego and are attached to form, sound, smell, taste, touch, and phenomena while engaging in giving, morality, and patience, then one will look for fame, praise, gain, and honor. A person with an attitude like this who does many good deeds may be reborn into a rich and wealthy family, or be reborn into a heavenly realm to experience immeasurable fortune and happiness. But such an attitude is an obstruction to becoming a Buddha. Practicing to be a great bodhisattva begins with contemplating non-self.

Many chant the *Heart Sutra* every day. But practicing the teachings of the *Heart Sutra* is also a matter of realizing that the five aggregates are all empty, and in this sense the *Heart Sutra* is not a particularly special or unique teaching. Contemplating non-self is a unified path, practiced by both arhats and bodhisattvas. This much is for certain. The *Lotus Sutra* says, "There is only one vehicle. There are not two or three," this one vehicle is the vehicle of the Noble Eightfold Path. "Right view" from the Noble Eightfold Path is seeing how "all phenomena are without self-nature". Whether Mahāyāna or Theravāda, both share this principle. Everyone should experience this and confirm it for themselves.

The *Heart Sutra* teaches that by contemplating non-self we can overcome all suffering: "...realized the five aggregates are empty and was liberated from all suffering and hardship.... this is true and not false". The Buddha would not lie to us. The *Diamond Sutra* lays out the fundamental teaching and cultivation methods of Mahāyāna bodhisattvas. The sutra guides everyone, teaching that "all forms are illusory" and "that which turns away from all notions is called all Buddhas." This is the proper way to practice.

All things arise due to causes and conditions, and are thus called "conditioned phenomena." If something could come into being without other causes and conditions, and had the nature of emptiness from the beginning it could be called an "unconditioned phenomena." Conditioned phenomena are impermanent and change very quickly. They are as substantive as dreams, illusions, bubbles, or shadows. They last in a given state only as long as dew or a flash of lightning. Contemplating and seeing the world in this way accords with the Way and the nature of emptiness.

Develop at Rest, Temper When Active

When learning Buddhism, we must come to understand the true form of the world. After attaining realization, we should continue to cultivate meditative concentration and uphold the precepts in everyday life. When such practices are combined with wisdom, we remove nervousness, impulsive actions, and habits. For example, when we encounter a sense object that pleases us, we will think about it constantly, generating defilement and infatuation. We also constantly think of those sense objects we hate or feel aversion towards, triggering habits of dislike. When unpleasant conditions suddenly appear we might curse or some other unwholesome behaviors may manifest.

In a meditation hall, we develop ourselves while at rest and temper ourselves while active. By quietly cultivating meditative concentration and habitual adherence to the precepts, we brighten the mind and see into our true nature. First, we develop ourselves by cultivating wholesome habits. Next we reenter the world to interact with others, temper these habits, and test ourselves. Is the mind pure and clear? Do our thoughts and actions harm others? Do we know our thoughts this very moment? This is the process of "tempering while active."

Cultivating after realization means continuing to practice one step at a time. Only through interacting with others can you realize your habits and come to know your temperament. Are your habits easy or difficult for others to accept? The harder they are to accept, the greater the severity of your habits. If you are disrespected, you might become furious, thinking your dignity and self-esteem have been damaged. But "self-esteem" is just another word for "self-attachment."

We can only practice through interacting with others. Taking a bustling, lively environment as our place of practice affords us the opportunity to "temper ourselves when active." In a meditation hall, we should diligently cultivate and maintain self-awareness and self-composure at all times. This is crucial. All things are impermanent. We should all exert ourselves in developing the habit of meditative concentration.

Only then can we maintain self-awareness when the mind arises and thoughts surface. This is a vital skill in all times and locations.

Chapter Nine

FUNDAMENTAL VERSES ON
THE MIDDLE WAY

Phenomena arise from causes and conditions,
I say they are emptiness.
They are also given an illusory name,
And also called the Middle Way.

A bove is a well-known verse from the *Fundamental Verses on the Middle Way*, a treatise written by the great second-century Mahāyāna Buddhist commentator Nāgārjuna. In fact, the verse forms the basis of the "one mind, three views" doctrine of the Tiantai School of Chinese Buddhism.

One Mind, Three Views

The doctrine of "one mind, three views" (一心三觀) is a foundational aspect of the Tiantai School of Chinese Buddhism. It teaches us to look at all phenomena with three perspectives: seeing phenomena as empty, seeing phenomena as illusory, and seeing phenomena as the Middle Way, which is a synthesis of the two.

Phenomena Arise from Causes and Conditions

The teaching on causes and conditions is a truth verified by the Buddha after surveying the world, not some imaginatively conjured point of philosophy. All phenomena, living or non-living, sentient or insentient, are all composed of more than two causes or conditions. Different combinations of causes and conditions produce different results. In the Buddha's teachings, this combination is referred to as a "unified form."

Ordinary people take these constructs of causes and conditions and believe them to be real, tangible things. This leads to defilement and attachment as people covet and pursue these constructs, producing all sorts of wholesome and unwholesome karma. The most important part of learning Buddhism is the ability to see through the illusory things of the world. Once practitioners see beyond illusion, they will find their true form, their "original face."

For example, when someone wants to write a book, the book first occurs as a stream of thoughts. Then, those thoughts are written down with a pen, computer, typewriter, or other such causes and conditions until a written draft is produced. That draft then goes through a printing press and is bound into a book. The direct causes and conditions that produced the book are things like the author's research, intellect, and literary skill. The book also has many indirect causes and conditions, like the causes and conditions that allowed the author to be born in this world, as well as the causes and conditions that led the author to become knowledgeable in his or her field of study.

The production of a book requires many causes and conditions to come together before it is completed. As it is dependent on causes and conditions, it is easy to see that it has no "self," and is entirely dependent. It is not completed by itself, but instead depends on the combination of many causes and conditions to become complete.

Everything in the world requires at least two causes and conditions to arise. Living things are included in this as well, for they require a mother and father to be born.

The *Fundamental Verses on the Middle Way* states that, "Phenomena arise from causes and conditions." "Causes" are the primary factors that shape an effect, and "conditions" are the factors which come together to help give rise to the effect. Simply put, causes and conditions come together and produce effects. Thus, all phenomena are effects.

Consider for a moment a meditation hall. It too is an effect. For the meditation hall to have been built, there must have been a cause. On one level, the land it rests upon can be seen as the cause, and the materials, blueprints, and labor to build the hall are all conditions. Only when all of these things come together can the meditation hall come into being.

As another example, Fo Guang Shan Monastery was bought forty years ago by Venerable Master Hsing Yun from the sale of a Buddhist Gift Shop in the city. In this way, Venerable Master Hsing Yun was the cause, his followers were the conditions, and the establishment of a monastery on this mountain was the effect.

Everything is like this: there is a primary cause that is paired with various conditions to produce an effect. Whether the effect arises from two simultaneous causes, or the causes come together successively, there are always multiple factors involved. This is the meaning of the verse, "Phenomena arise from causes and conditions."

I Say They Are Emptiness

Considering all the effects produced by causes and conditions, the Buddha's teachings say they are "emptiness." Because effects are produced through causes and conditions it is said that they are "empty" of any true, substantial existence, and are "empty" of any inherent essence. In this sense, they cannot be said to be truly in-dependent, truly unchanging, or truly real. Individual causes and conditions exist in relation to their surroundings, and are constantly changing because of outside influence.

For example, suppose we are in a room which is newly carpet-ed. At first, when people walked around on the uncarpeted floor, it made noise which disturbed the peaceful atmosphere. This became a condition which presented a new need, and the room is now car-peted. Needs like this arise all the time, and become the causes and conditions of future effects. All past and future causes and effects mutually influence one another. Another example is the environ-ment. Our current concern with environmental protection is a re-sponse to environmental problems that arose because of humanity's previous actions which did not care for the environment.

Since everything arises from causes and conditions, everything lacks self-nature. All things depend on causes and conditions to be as they are. For instance, plastic products vary depending on the molds they are poured into, becoming household appliances, industrial prod-ucts, or materials for construction. In each case, the conditions are dif-ferent. It is like a factory receiving a change in its equipment and man-agement. As conditions change, so too do the effects they produce.

We can see that all phenomena arise from causes and conditions and do not have independent natures. After phenomena arise, they are influenced by their surroundings, ensuring that they go through constant change. Eventually, they come apart and are destroyed. But this process isn't truly destruction, for energy returns to energy and matter returns to matter. In some cases, two differing materials split from one another and join with other compatible materials, becom-ing something new.

Everything becomes as it is under the constantly changing influ-ence of causes and conditions. They may become like this or like that, but all the while they lack self-nature. This is the Buddha's teaching; and lacking self-nature is the same as having the nature of emptiness.

Buddhism has been in China for over two thousand years, and as such it has seeped deeply into the daily lives of Chinese people, such that everyone understands at least a little bit of the Dharma. That said, they may not understand true reality. The most important part of studying Buddhism is to come to know the true form of the universe. To see these truths, view all things through the teaching of dependent origination. Only then will you see through illusion. See past illusion, and you can attain enlightenment. Then you will realize that there is no arising or ceasing.

They Are Also Given an Illusory Name

Since all in the world is created through causes and conditions, all are merely illusory forms. Only the following can thereby be concluded:

Everything is Uncertain

Once causes and conditions give rise to an effect, that construct is able to influence others, and can be influenced by outside things as well. Thereafter, it undergoes constant change. There are no fixed or permanent "effects." The notion that "all conditioned phenomena are impermanent" may be easy to teach to others with the hope that it can comfort them in difficult times, but when a grave matter comes up it is not so easy to simply let go. Why? Because the notion that "all conditioned phenomena are impermanent" is not knowledge we gained for ourselves. We do not yet have right view.

The teaching is still just some words in our ears or things we have seen. This is how we know emptiness. We have yet to contemplate dependent origination and deeply penetrate this view: *everything* arises through dependent origination and is subject to cause and effect. From existence to non-existence, from arising to cessation, from birth to death, everything is impermanent. To study Buddhism, it is necessary to first develop this right view. Only then can we hope to achieve liberation.

We may occasionally utter the phrase "the world is impermanent," but are we able to truly see it in our own lives? We should constantly reflect that "all conditioned phenomena are impermanent." Why? Because all phenomena arise through dependent origination, and are dependent upon causes and conditions. They do not manifest on their own, do not arise on their own, do not exist on their own, and are not complete on their own. All phenomena are illusory and impermanent. Since this is so, why are we attached to position and authority?

Consider attachment and desire. When we have desire, there is suffering. When we have no desire, there is happiness. As long as we have desire for something, we fear not getting it, and when we have it, we fear losing it. Thus we suffer. Desire is a form of delusional clinging. Since the world is an illusion, why bother pursuing desires? Such is a blind pursuit. If we gain authority, what will we do with it? In a few years, we will have to pass it on to someone else. Learning Buddhism allows us to understand dependent origination and the impermanence of the world. Only through this process can we let go of power, fame, status, and desire.

Let go, and we need not worry any more about gain or loss. Without worrying about gain or loss, we will be at ease. If we use the teaching of dependent origination to see reality as it is, then we can be at ease just like Avalokitesvara Bodhisattva, whose name in Chinese is *guan zizai* (觀自在), "observing at ease." We all want to feel at ease, right? Only through understanding dependent origination can we be like this. Dependent origination is the way to liberation from birth and death, and a direct way to feeling at ease in this very moment. This is the truth the Buddha was enlightened to.

Nothing is Independent

What in this world can be called independent? In order to have a "self," something must exercise agency and be independent. People are made of both physical and mental components. Physically a person can be divided into earth, water, fire, and wind. Mentally, a person can be divided into feeling, perception, mental formations, and consciousness. When the physical elements of form are combined with these mental elements, they make up the five aggregates. In whatever the five aggregates are present we call a "sentient being."

Human beings are not independent. When a person dies, earth, water, fire, and wind each return from whence they came. Feeling perception, mental formations, and consciousness return to consciousness, until they each take on another name and form. This continues from lifetime to lifetime. Consciousness is simply our accumulated physical, verbal, and mental actions. They are converted from matter into energy in the infinite and boundless storehouse of memories. Since we are dependently originated, we are not truly real.

If you can see that all conditioned phenomena are impermanent, then all worldly pleasures of form, sound, smell, taste, and touch, the five desires of wealth, sex, fame, food and drink, and sleep, and the lust between men and women lose their appeal and are let go of. In this way, we are liberated from the five desires and lust in this life, and can be at ease.

And Also Called the Middle Way

The *Heart Sutra* teaches us to contemplate everything as created through conditions and as empty in nature. Earth, water, fire, and wind are not real, and the forms that they make up are also not real. Their nature is empty and lacks a self. So too are all the myriad things of the world with their different forms and appearances. This

"emptiness" is embedded in the physical world. That is the philosophy of the "Middle Way."

The science of physics describes an atom as made up of electrons,
protons, and neutrons. Differing numbers of these atomic particles
produce objects of different states, shapes, and functions. Accord-
ingly, we give them different names. Everything follows causes and
conditions. Some things become like this, others become like that.
As such they have different states, sizes, functions, and effects. All
things are illusions, arising and ceasing according to conditions.
They are not real.

All phenomena arise from conditions, and are empty in nature.
Form and emptiness are the same. Form is emptiness and emptiness
is form. Those who are able to see through illusion and falsehood
can realize that all things lack a self-nature that is independent and
unchanging. Consequently, one understands that illusory phenomena are not real and are subject to arising, abiding, change, and cessation. Nothing that arises is eternal and unchanging. The *Heart Sutra*
refers to this as "they do not arise or cease."

Consider the sky. How clouds vanish or reappear has little influence on the sky itself. The open space remains empty, neither
pure nor impure. Within true reality, all phenomena do not arise or
cease, are neither defiled nor pure, and do not increase nor decrease.
Awaken to this and you enter *nirvāṇa*. There is only tranquility.
Even though we use terms like "formation, abiding, destruction, and
void," and "arising, abiding, change, cessation" to describe the way
things change, these terms do not describe true reality.

The sutras say, "To see dependent origination is to see the Dharma. To see the Dharma is to see the Buddha." If we understand
dependent origination and see through illusion, we can enter true
reality. See how all phenomena arise due to conditions and lack
independent self-nature, then one will see the Dharma nature of all

phenomena. The final goal of practicing meditative concentration and the final goal of brightening the mind and seeing our true nature is the same as the goal of taking refuge in the Dharma and in *nirvāṇa*.

The highest method of learning Buddhism is to take refuge in the Dharma and take refuge in *nirvāṇa*. *Nirvāṇa* is the true form of all phenomena: neither arising nor ceasing, neither pure nor defiled, neither increasing nor decreasing. First, practitioners should continually examine the world through dependent origination, cultivating the view that "all conditioned phenomena are impermanent" and "all phenomena are without self-nature". Not only will practitioners achieve liberation and freedom unto themselves, they will also shed their desire for worldly things. Gradually they will exist in union with the true form of *nirvāṇa*, and enter the realm of *nirvāṇa*'s perfect tranquility.

When we adopt this view as our own, we have achieved "right view." This is the stage of "renunciation" on the path to liberation. When one renounces the three realms, the five desires, and worldly phenomena, one enters the way of renouncing the world.

Eliminating Birth and Death

Liberation from birth and death is possible through examination of dependent origination. When the six sense organs come into contact with sense objects, "contact" is made, leading to "feeling." With the arising of "feeling" we develop "craving." With "craving" comes "clinging." With "clinging" comes "becoming." With "becoming" comes "birth." With "birth" comes "old age and death." This is the way to the cycle of birth and death, as shown by dependent origination.

When we look into the way that leads to *nirvāṇa*, the six sense organs make "contact" with sense objects, but instead give rise to the mind of renunciation, which no longer exhibits worldly desires. With the cessation of "contact" comes the cessation of "feeling." With the cessation of "feeling" comes the cessation of "craving." With the cessation of "craving" comes the cessation of "clinging." With the cessation of "clinging" comes the cessation of "becoming." With the cessation of "becoming" comes the cessation of "birth." With the cessation of "birth" comes the cessation of "old age and death," and all forms of suffering. One is thus liberated and attains *nirvāṇa*.

Language requires thought to come into being. When the mind is disturbed, we cry out. Views arise when we experience "contact" and "feeling," leading to imagination and analysis. Ultimately, this becomes language. Because of this, language too is subject to dependent origination. It does not have an inherent self-nature. Our thoughts pass through the six sense organs before they are discerned in the mind. Thought is also subject to dependent origination and lacks self-nature. Even our physical actions depend on external causes and conditions to arise.

All spoken language, written words, ideas, and worldly phenomena are illusions. They are all subject to dependent origination. Because there is this, there is that. Because this arises, that arises. After true reality is understood, you see that all phenomena are illusory, and that nothing arises or ceases. Understand this and you will no longer cling to such illusory things, and avoid the behaviors that arise from clinging. You will no longer generate karma.

By developing meditative concentration and putting an end to karma, we will no longer be lead to future rebirth. Understanding true reality is *prajñā*-wisdom, which is the same as "brightening the mind." Once we mistook worldly things to be real. This is ignorance. By brightening the mind with wisdom, we remove clinging to illusions, delusional thinking, and ignorance. Liberation from birth and death then becomes a possibility.

Closely examine all things in this world. To develop this view, take "All mundane phenomena are illusory" as your *huatou*. Allow it to give rise to doubt and direct your thinking. Study it frequently. "All mundane phenomena are illusory." Remember the line from the *Diamond Sutra*: "All conditioned phenomena are like dreams, illusions, bubbles, or shadows." Each of these is an example of an illusory phenomena. Recite this *huatou* often. Let it become your catchphrase. In this way you can be free of external things. As your meditative concentration develops and you are on the cusp of entering *samādhi*, about to enter *dhyāna*, or have attained the *dhyāna* states, you will naturally develop this kind of wisdom without outflows.

Use this wisdom without outflows and see into all worldly illusions. See how they lack an independent self nature. This is what it means to use non-discriminating wisdom to see the world of non-discrimination. In the end, by fully realizing this concept and completely transcending the body, one thereby attains inner transcendence. You will gain the realization mentioned by the *Heart Sutra*: "All phenomena are empty. They do not arise or extinguish, are not defiled or pure, do not increase or decrease." When you are able to see with wisdom that all things are without an independent self-nature, you will be able to enter the unified form in which "there is no wisdom and no attainment."

After understanding dependent origination, you can fully know what it means to let go. As human beings, in the end we have nothing. "You may own a thousand homes, but you can only sleep in one bed. Your wealth may contain ten thousand treasures, but you can only eat three meals a day." When we are born, we arrive with no possessions. When we die, we can't bring anything with us. The world is a chaotic spiral. In the end, nothing is settled or resolved. Is there anything you can take with you? So let it go! Only by letting go can you truly be free.

Chapter Ten

A LIFE OF LIBERATION

Reading the Heart Sutra

The *Heart Sutra* is the most commonly read religious text in China. Among all Buddhist sutras, the *Heart Sutra* contains the most essential wisdom. Though it is little more than two hundred and fifty characters in length, it is a complete exposition of the path of practice.

Chinese Buddhists recite the *Heart Sutra* during their morning and evening chanting. The *Heart Sutra* is also chanted at temple Dharma services to liberate those who have passed away. The sutra is chanted with the intention that the merit will help beings be re-born in the Western Pure Land of Amitābha Buddha. However, few people know that the *Heart Sutra* is a priceless treasure that can help them in this very life. The purpose of the sutra is to liberate us from suffering, remove obstacles and worries, and allow us to be at ease every day.

The *Heart Sutra* and *Diamond Sutra* both teach us to see through, and let go of illusion. As such, both sutras emphasize emptiness, and discuss it in-depth. The *Eight Realizations of a Bodhisattva Sutra,*

Heart Sutra

Avalokitesvara Bodhisattva, while contemplating deeply the *prajñāparamita*, realized the five aggregates are empty and was liberated from all suffering and hardship.

Sariputra, form is not different from emptiness, emptiness is not different from form. Form is emptiness. Emptiness is form. The same is true of feeling, perception, mental formations, and consciousness.

Sariputra, all phenomena are empty. They do not arise or cease, are not defiled or pure, do not increase or decrease. Thus, in emptiness, there are no forms, feelings, perceptions, mental formations, or consciousness.

No eye, ear, nose, tongue, body, or mind; no form, sound, smell, taste, touch or *dharmas;* no eye consciousness so on unto mind consciousness; no ignorance and extinction of ignorance; even unto no aging and death and no extinction of aging and death; no suffering, cause of suffering, cessation, or path; no wisdom and no attainment.

As there is no attainment, bodhisattvas who rely on the *prajñāparamita* have neither worry nor obstruction. Without worry and obstruction, there is no fear. Away from confusion and delusion, they will ultimately reach *nirvāna.* All the Buddhas of the past, present, and future rely on the *prajñāparamita* to attain *anuttara-samyak-sambodhi.*

Thus, know that the *prajñāparamita* is the great profound mantra, is the illuminating mantra, is the most supreme of all mantras, is the unequalled mantra, able to eliminate all suffering, is true and not false.

Thus, proclaim the *"Prajñāparamita Mantra,"* proclaim the mantra that says:

Gate gate paragate parasamgate bodhi svaha.

which was taught to the great bodhisattvas, emphasizes impermanence even more strongly. Though it is even shorter than the *Heart Sutra*, it contains the phrase "birth and death" seven times! The sutra mentions "impermanence," that "nations are dangerous and fragile," and teaches bodhisattvas to contemplate impermanence, non-self, suffering, and emptiness in their daily lives. The development of this kind of wisdom is especially emphasized in Humanistic Buddhism. Mahāyāna bodhisattvas strive to cultivate both merit and wisdom. However, a practitioner who wishes to successfully cultivate both merit and wisdom must first ensure that they have the correct understanding of wisdom.

A Summary of the Heart Sutra's Teachings

The *Heart Sutra* teaches us to leave behind suffering and attain happiness. Leaving behind suffering can be read in the passage, "… without worry and obstruction, there is no fear. Away from confusion and delusion…." Attaining happiness is represented by Avalokitesvara Bodhisattva. The key to spiritual cultivation is to remove the attachment to the self, which can be seen in the passage "realized the five aggregates are empty."

Emptiness of the Five Aggregates

This world is full of suffering. Suffering takes many forms: the suffering of birth, old age, sickness, and death, being separated from loved ones, not getting what we want, and being near loathsome people as well as many other kinds of suffering. These kinds of mental suffering stem from attachment to unskillful thinking. They originate from the belief in a "self" that is independent and real. If we wish to leave behind suffering and attain happiness, we must first see the five aggregates as empty. Only then can we be rid of the various forms of suffering, like birth, old age, sickness, and death, being separated from loved ones, and being near loathsome people. After we use *prajñā*-wisdom to see that the five aggregates are empty, we can leave behind confusion and delusion, and be free from fear.

Confusion, Delusion, and Fear

Why does the *Heart Sutra* say that by giving up delusion and confusion, we are free from fear? First of all, we should look into what people are afraid of. Whether it be workers or students, most people face obstacles regarding their futures. They are afraid that their prospects are bleak, that they may get hurt, not get their way, or experience other such problems.

Why does the *Diamond Sutra* state that "the mind of the future cannot be obtained?" This is because worldly causes and conditions are difficult to explain. The future could change at any time. Nothing can be predicted with perfect certainty. Since it is impossible to predict what has yet to happen, we should stop trying to forecast the future. Instead, we should focus on the here and now, and take hold of the present moment.

Most people do not understand the meaning of "the mind of the future cannot be obtained." They are constantly worrying and being held back. If we analyze the origin of these worries and obstacles, we will see that they all originate from attachment to the self. We need *prajñā*-wisdom in order to leave worries and obstacles behind. Then we have nothing to fear.

Confusion and delusion are a kind of "idle chatter." They are not real, but we take them to be real. For example, the mind frequently manifests various illusory thoughts. Whether it is nostalgia for past events or old friends, such thoughts are pleasant sense objects. As soon as you think of these things, the mind follows these sense objects deep into fantasy.

These fantasies are not real, and are unlikely to become real. Such thoughts are confusion and delusion. All people produce a ceaseless stream of deluded thoughts that float up to the forefront of the mind. This is known as "idle chatter." People continue to fantasize because they have a concept of a self. With *prajñā*-wisdom they can remove the attachment to the self, and leave confusion and delusion behind.

Contemplating at Ease

The *Heart Sutra* opens with the Chinese name of Avalokiteśvara Bodhisattva, *guan zizai* (觀自在), which means "contemplating at ease." This is the epitome of fearlessness. Not being able to obtain the people, events, objects, and situations we favor causes us to suffer and feel fear. This is because the "self" longs after these things. If we wish to be free from fear, we must devote ourselves to the *"prajñā* of contemplation."

These are not merely shallow words. Contemplate phenomena deeply. See how they are made of causes and conditions. See how they are not real. See how they are illusions. Contemplate in this way until you eradicate all attachment to the phenomena of the world. Only by removing the attachment to the self can you not be entranced by external sense objects. This kind of understanding is the *"prajñā* of contemplation."

Someone with this understanding contemplates and sees how all things with the world are illusory. Seeing sense objects in this way as they arise is referred to in the *Heart Sutra* as "contemplating deeply the *prajñāparamita*." Those who can consistently contemplate in deep *prajñāparamita* can be without affliction, whether they encounter beloved, detested, worrisome, or obstructing sense objects.

If you want to directly experience how all worldly phenomena are illusory, first ask yourself: is the "self" real or not? What we call the self is actually an illusion as well. It is simply a combination of the five aggregates of form, feelings, perception, mental formations, and consciousness. If even one of those elements change, the resulting "self" is different from the previous "self." This "self" is subject to constant, continual change. It is influenced by its environment. The present "self" is just a temporary illusion. The "self" is empty.

At first, we all mistakenly believe that the five aggregates are not empty, that the "self" is real and unchanging. We fear not getting what the "self" wants, and even if the "self" gets such things, we fear losing them. This is why the key to deeply contemplating *prajñāparamita* is to see the five aggregates as empty.

What is Prajñā?

Developing *prajñā* can be divided into the three stages of "wisdom from hearing," "wisdom from thinking," and "wisdom from practice." There is a Buddhist saying, "When worldly desires shrink by a foot, the Way grows by a foot." If you understand this saying, you will open your eyes and see through the illusion of the world. To have this kind of understanding, you must be able to transform all that you hear into wisdom. This means understanding dependent origination and the three Dharma seals.

"Wisdom from thinking" is rarely practiced by people, because most people find it difficult to be at ease. Those who want to bring their spiritual practice into their daily lives should develop "wisdom from thinking." "Wisdom from thinking" is also known as "right thought" in the Noble Eightfold Path. Practitioners should use all they have learned in Buddhism to contemplate and think about the world, examining all phenomena in great details. From this they will realize that all things are impermanent, without an independent self, and are subject to cause and effect. Gradually, this will seep into their worldview. This is "right view" within the Noble Eightfold Path. After their meditative concentration has reached the point of entering *samādhi*, the truth of the three Dharma seals can be experienced directly. Only then can such people be said to have developed "wisdom from practice."

The Universality of Dependent Origination

The word "*prajñā*" in the *Heart Sutra* means "wisdom." This kind of wisdom corresponds to "right view" within the Noble Eightfold Path. The Mahāyāna bodhisattvas have a high level of wisdom, and are able to directly observe the empty nature of all things. They understand the interdependent relationships between causes and conditions that give rise to phenomena. They know that phenomena do not have an unchanging, fixed nature. Their essence is empty. For bodhisattvas, "right view" is seeing emptiness in this way. By comparison, for arhats, "right view" is seeing dependent origination. It is through a deep understanding of dependent origination that arhats become enlightened.

Dependent origination is based on the principle that "when this arises, that arises." "Arise" simply means to come into being. When causes and conditions arise and join, effects arise. Another central principle of dependent origination is, "when this exists, that exists." This refers to when causes and conditions are already extant, and effects exist in response. The first principle emphasizes the process of how effects arise, and the second emphasizes the period when they are already present.

All causes and conditions arise due to other causes and conditions. Even when they fall apart, and their every component is destroyed, they will continue to influence the future. Whether it is air pollution, environmental pollution, or something else entirely, they all abide by the principle that "When this arises, that arises. When this exists, that exists." Practitioners who examine dependent origination will see that the world is impermanent, lacks any self-nature, and that it exhibits the perfect tranquility of *nirvāna*. Using this wisdom to examine the world is called "the contemplation of emptiness."

For example, take a look at the alarm clock that sits upon your nightstand and consider it as an "effect." The batteries, wires, plastic framework, and all the other component parts are all causes and conditions. Probe into any of these individual components and you will see that they too are effects, formed by their own causes and conditions. For instance, how was the clock's plastic shell made? It was created through some plastic material and a particular mold. With the plastic and the mold as required factors, the plastic shell could be made.

The plastic material used for the clock's shell is also an effect. It was smelted in chemical factories and oil refineries. It is possible to apply the logic of "When this arises, that arises," as far back as you want. In a related example, oil makes possible the manufacturing of plastic products, paint, and tar. All products take their shape through a process of construction and continuous change.

After an effect arises, it combines with other elements in the surrounding environment, becoming something new. This new, changed effect continues to combine with its surroundings, becoming new again and again. This process of development carries on continually in accordance with dependent origination.

Through the union of parents and the *ālaya* consciousness, new beings take shape. The father and mother provide the material basis for a new life form (the combination of sperm and egg becoming a zygote). After that, consciousness combines with that material being. From that point onward, the mother provides nourishment, and the fetus slowly undergoes gestation until it is born.

After the infant is born, events continue to unfold in accordance with dependent origination, "When this arises, that arises. When this exists, that exists." For example, breast-feeding, changing diapers, and other such child rearing activities are essential. Without this care, the infant could not continue existing. From birth until death, that child's body changes continuously. When death comes, the process of "When this ceases, that ceases" begins. Without the breath and body heat, the body begins rotting. Through careful contemplation of all things, we see how they all exist and change according to cause and effect.

Impermanence

Now that you understand the workings of cause and effect, can you see how nothing in the world is set in stone? All phenomena are moving forward and changing, this is just the way things are.

With change, nothing is set in stone. For that reason we should look at everything in the world, power and desire most especially, and be able to see their drawbacks and let them go. Suppose we pursue power with great fervor and manage to obtain it, it will not be long before things change and the power is passed on to someone else. It is unfortunate that ordinary people foolishly think, "It's a term. Even if it's just three or four years, I'd still be willing!" Such people are led by attachment. They do not stop to think about how quickly time passes. At most, one may serve for six years, ten years, or perhaps more than ten. But power is something that will unquestionably vanish at some point.

The CEO of the Fo Guang Shan Foundation for Buddhist Culture and Education, Venerable Tzu Hui, often reminds everyone to maintain a sense of alertness. For Buddhists, true alertness means awareness of impermanence. This includes the doctrine of "non-self." Most Chinese Buddhists think that the teaching "all conditioned phenomena are impermanent and all phenomena are without self-nature" is too passive, but they are mistaken to dismiss this teaching.

Non-Self

Dependent origination is defined as: "When this arises, that arises. When this exists, that exists. When this ceases, that ceases."

"When this arises" and "when this exists" refer to the products of causes and conditions. In other words, all things have at least two qualifying conditions. But even if the constituent elements are the same, when the process by which they come together differs, the effect will differ as well. For example, gold can be beaten into a ring or an earring. Even though gold is materially the same as the resulting ring or earring, it had to be heated and softened to a proper smelting temperature. Different processes of preparing the gold allow it to be pounded into a ring or an earring. Everything takes shape through two or more qualifying conditions.

The "self" in the phrase "all phenomena are without self-nature," is not the same self we refer to when using words like "I," "you," "he," or "she." "Self" refers to an independent nature which is not controlled by other things. Consider a person who is controlled by another person. Immediately that person would feel a loss of freedom. This person could be ordered to laugh, cry, or do anything, and they would have to obey. In this case, independence would be freedom from that control. Independence means that we can be at ease; for without this kind of freedom ease is not possible.

Those who have their own independence but exercise control over others are usually called rulers or kings. A king's power is truly great. Not only does a king reign supremely, but he can make life or death decisions. Furthermore, they can have whatever they want. Take the first emperor of China, Qín Shǐ Huáng, as an example. Though he sent subjects out to seek the elixir of immortality for him, he had other subjects begin the construction of his mausoleum. His mausoleum was not made after his death, but was built during his lifetime. He wanted both: the elixir of life, and an ornate mausoleum. But even though he was a mighty ruler, he had no control over life and death.

Consider the universal law that "When this arises, that arises." Can anything truly be independent? Your own body and mind are mutually dependent. They cannot be separated from one another. Even if he or she is in good health, when a person's spirits are down, they become lazy and lethargic. In much the same manner, a person might be enthusiastic or spirited, but his or her body is too ill to move. The mind and body are tied to one another. Neither is in control.

Human existence binds together body and mind. Without a self, they cannot be independent. In the past, people used to think that, "You should not speak of impermanence and non-self. They're too negative and pessimistic!" Śākyamuni Buddha examined all worldly phenomena through dependent origination. He did not differentiate between animate or inanimate, sentient or insentient. He found they were all mutually interdependent and in a constant state of change. Nothing in the world is fixed. His goal was to point out the supramundane truths of cause and effect and dependent origination. Nothing is certain. He wanted us to recognize the world as it truly is. This view is neither extreme nor pessimistic. It is the truth of the world.

We shouldn't say, "Talking about impermanence and non-self all day long is so negative!" Everything in the world lacks a self-nature. Nothing is independent. Seeing things like this is the only way to be at ease. This view is natural and direct, and we should work to transform it from conception to the way we live.

When you look at something, you may find it attractive. In worldly terms, we can discern good and bad qualities. Compare things and you will find some refined and others coarse, some attractive and others ugly. Even though their appearance is illusory, these perceived differences cannot be denied.

When you are taken by something that is attractive, refined, or useful, quickly direct your attention inward and examine it with your mind. "That is illusory. It is not real. Once causes and conditions change, it will no longer be as attractive or useful as it is now."

Otherwise, after the moment passes the mind will continue to long for that object and think about it. This is craving.

What is craving? Suppose you encounter some sense object and, afterwards, your mind is completely subsumed by it. You can't get rid of it. While you are walking, eating, and sleeping, you will keep thinking about it. As soon as your eyes open, or when you are no longer busy with something, you will think about it. This is craving.

The fundamental reason the mind is consumed by craving is because of the "self." It is essential to frequently reflect that "all conditioned phenomena are impermanent" and "all phenomena are without self-nature," which is to say they are not independent and autonomous. Examine things in this way and you will no longer be seduced by external sense objects. What you mistake to be real is not real. We believe there is a "self" which can acquire things, and therefore we try to attain external sense objects.

Chan masters often say, "Like a scarecrow gazing upon flowers and birds, how could he be hindered by all surrounding phenomena?" and "Passing through one hundred flowers in a dense forest, no petals or leaves cling to the body." A person must have *prajñā* wisdom in order to possess this state of mind.

Nirvāna is Perfect Tranquility

We should cultivate right view and see the world according to dependent origination and cause and effect. After analyzing the world in this way, we can see that everything is indeed constantly changing and is just as impermanent as we've described. If we go further and see our own daily lives in this way, slowly it will become our own personal view. You will come to see that "all conditioned phenomena are impermanent" and "all phenomena are without self-nature." All things are insubstantial and empty.

"Impermanence" is the nature of emptiness. "Non-Self" is also the nature of emptiness. This world is empty. Even the planet, which has existed for ages, continues to turn and change. One day, even this planet will be destroyed. After all, it too is an illusion.

By viewing things through dependent origination, we can see that all things are illusions. Underneath this illusion their nature is empty. Nothing we can see truly arises or ceases, comes or goes, is pure or impure, and does not increase or decrease. The true form of phenomena is described by the phrase "*nirvāṇa* is perfect tranquility." Conventionally, worldly phenomena are impermanent, changing, and bound by dependent origination. In this way they are "conditioned phenomena." But when we look at such phenomena's intrinsic nature we can see that they are empty, without a self, do not arise or cease, and do not come or go. From this perspective they are "unconditioned phenomena." In this way emptiness is not separate or different from worldly existence.

These are the three Dharma seals: "all conditioned phenomena are impermanent," "all phenomena are without self-nature," and "*nirvāṇa* is perfect tranquility." Many Buddhists may say things like, "Oh, the three Dharma seals? If something is in line with the three Dharma seals, it can be taken as the Buddha's teachings." This is true, but is also an oversimplification. How then can people attain liberation?

An Explication of the Heart Sutra

1. Avalokiteśvara Bodhisattva

If we use *prajñā*-wisdom in our everyday tasks, the mind will no longer be nervous, worried, or obstructed. In other words, we will not have fear, confusion, or delusion. This is living at ease, and the *Heart Sutra* can lead us to this kind of life. The first three characters of the *Heart Sutra* are *guan zizai* (觀自在), the Chinese name of

Avalokiteśvara Bodhisattva, but they also literally mean "contemplating at ease." These first three characters do not necessarily only refer to Avalokiteśvara Bodhisattva the individual—they also encourage us to seek a life that is free and at ease.

The first character, *guan* (觀), means to contemplate or observe. If desire arises for external sense objects, look within and ask yourself, "Is the object I desire real?" Use the Buddha's teachings and contemplate: "To become as it is now, causes and conditions came together to create a unified form. In the future it will continue to change and fade away." For this reason you should not cling so tightly. If you keep recollecting that there is nothing you need to cling to, you will not care if you do obtain the sense object. There is no need to be concerned. Being unconcerned is being at ease. Living life in this way is called "following conditions," which is being at ease and knowing that all things arise and cease according to causes and conditions. Consider: are the conditions present for me to get what I want? If the conditions are simply not there, then let it go. You need not expend all your energy pursuing that effect. If there are sufficient causes and conditions, then go right ahead, but do not be too attached. After all, causes and conditions will one day come apart. The *Heart Sutra* is indeed wonderfully in touch with human life.

2. While Contemplating Deeply the Prajñāparamita

Bodhisattvas are extremely direct. Because they see things according to dependent origination, they understand that the world is empty. This is what is called "contemplating deeply the *prajñāparamita*."

"Dependent origination" means that phenomena arise depending on causes and conditions. A main cause combines with some secondary conditions and an effect is produced. All beings, objects, and events require two or more causes and conditions to arise. According to the universal law of cause and effect, among everything we can see, hear, or think about, nothing is completely independent and self-reliant. Everything depends on causes and conditions. Nothing is unchanging. In Buddhism, we say that things lack "self-nature," which is another way of saying they are empty.

Something with "self-nature" would be able to exist of its own accord. It would exist independent of everything else, and remain unchanging forever. All things that lack self-nature are called "conditioned phenomena," because they require causes and conditions to exist. If there was something that did not arise dependent on causes and conditions and could exist forever unchanging, it would be an "unconditioned phenomena." Two examples of such phenomena are emptiness itself and *nirvāṇa*.

Can people understand that everything is illusory, that nothing is independently arisen, real, or stable? This is the truth of the world. It doesn't matter if this view is considered "passive" or "extreme." To "contemplate deeply the *prajñāparamita*" means to use this concept to observe the world and see that all things are illusory.

3. Realized the five aggregates are empty

The Middle Way does not lean towards emptiness, nor does it learn towards existence. To put it another way, it is not biased towards the physical or the mental. Emptiness means knowing that phenomena are not real, not independent, and not eternal. After enlightenment, we can understand that the true nature of phenomena is emptiness. Form and emptiness cannot be differentiated from one another. The *Heart Sutra* states: "Form is not different from emptiness, emptiness is not different from form." This is how the sutra walks the Middle Way.

The other four aggregates, feeling, perception, mental formations, and consciousness, are the same. They arise dependent on causes and conditions. "Feeling" refers to the sensations that are produced when the six sense organs come into contact with sense objects. They arise through dependent origination, and do not exist on their own. Depending on your mood, contact with a sense object may generate a different feeling, pleasant or unpleasant. Feelings are not fixed experiences, they change and vary depending on your moods and emotions.

Perception also arises through dependent origination. Contact occurs and feelings arise. After feeling arises then analysis, categorization, and consolidation take place. Thus perception also lacks self-nature. Mental formations are how we make decisions. They depend upon the previous aggregate of perception to decide upon a course of action. Mental formations also lack self-nature, and arise based on dependent origination. Consciousness is the accumulated memories of physical, verbal, and mental behaviors. Memory also lacks self-nature.

Feeling, perception, mental formations, and consciousness all lack self-nature. It is not simply that "Form is not different from emptiness, emptiness is not different from form." It could also be said that, "Feeling is not different from emptiness, emptiness is not different from feeling," "Perception is not different from emptiness, emptiness is not different from perception," "Mental formations are not different from emptiness, emptiness is not different from mental formations," and "Consciousness is not different from emptiness, emptiness is not different from consciousness." In the *Heart Sutra*, this is simplified as "The same is true of feeling, perception, mental formations, and consciousness." Therefore, the five aggregates are all empty.

4. And Was Liberated from All Suffering and Hardship

Non-Buddhists may say, "You Buddhists have no drive! The way you think has no competitiveness!" I wish to tell everyone, it is only

136 Meditation and Wisdom

through the drive to be liberated from suffering and hardship that we become accomplished. This is true Buddhism.

Only liberation from suffering and hardship makes us unbeatable. Even if other people don't like you, don't be moved by insult and slander. If you are an average, ordinary person, no one will envy you. But if you are extremely talented and have great ability you will be celebrated by those who have a positive affinity with you, and detested by those who have a negative affinity. Such people will think of many ways to attack or slander you—things have always been this way.

If you want to be diligent and successful, it is only by practicing the Buddha's teachings that you can be free from fear of criticism, attack, insult, slander, or harm. All these things lack self-nature. They are empty and insubstantial. This is what Śākyamuni Buddha taught us. Understand these truths and you can stand up to hardship, move forward, and not fear harm from others. This is why, in Fo Guang Shan, we say, "Where there is Dharma, there is a way." The Buddha's teachings provide a worldview that can guide your behavior and help you make decisions. This is the process of cultivation. How could one say that Humanistic Buddhism lacks drive? How could it be called passive?

5. Form Is Not Different from Emptiness

When sentient beings are mired in confusion, they look for something unchanging they can hold on to. "Self" is defined as something that is in control of its own actions, free, and unrestricted. However, everything and every happening is a combination of conditions and causes. They are not directed by human will. For example, an infant will gradually change each day, growing and aging. The process doesn't stop. No one can maintain youth, health, intelligence, agility, or good fortune through sheer force of will. We cannot remain in transient states like youth, peak experiences, or good fortune. That is why we suffer.

By frequently contemplating dependent origination, we can see that the world is impermanent. Because it is impermanent, it brings us suffering. Because it brings suffering, it unquestionably lacks self-nature. It is not free, at ease, or happy. Arhats advanced towards liberation by contemplating dependent origination and impermanence. Through careful analysis they came to realize how all things within the world suffer and lack self-nature. In this way they attained liberation. This is described by the sutras as, "To see dependent origination is to see the Dharma, to see the Dharma is to see the Buddha."

In this context, "to see Dharma" means to see the empty nature of all phenomena. The wisdom of bodhisattvas is even greater than this, for they realize that dependent origination itself is also empty. Dependent origination is the principle that dictates how matter takes shape. Everything relies upon causes and conditions to be produced. When those causes and conditions separate, the effects they produced deteriorate and fall apart. Therefore the nature form, physical phenomena, is empty. "Form is not different from emptiness" means that matter and matter's empty nature are not different from one another. Bodhisattvas can see the empty nature of all sense objects they encounter.

To enter *nirvāṇa* Śākyamuni Buddha observed how all phenomena, including people, things, and events, arise and cease depending on causes and conditions. He had to understand illusion and see into the empty nature of all phenomena. The destination of all wisdom is seeing through the illusion of external things, and realizing that the universe lacks self-nature. The Buddha is wisdom embodied; this is the Buddha's "Dharma body." When the universe is viewed with wisdom, it is called the "Dharma realm."

6. Emptiness Is Not Different from Form

Physical phenomena, the "form" aggregate, is a combination of the four great elements of earth, water, fire, and wind. They represent the qualities of stability, cohesion, movement, and separation. Earth is secure and stable. Water assembles and creates cohesion. Wind causes the body to move and draws things inward. Fire ripens and separates, as it turns food into energy.

Everything in the universe is made up of these four great elements. The elements of earth, water, fire, and wind are not independent. They each rely upon the others, and it is through their mutual interdependence that they take shape as physical phenomena. If they are separated phenomena lose their shape, qualities, and function. Consequently physical phenomena are sometimes called "the emptiness of the four great elements."

The Buddha worried that people would hear that the world was empty and think it is not possible to become enlightened or attain liberation from birth and death. Non-Buddhists interpret "emptiness" as nihilism. They think that "emptiness" is nothingness. This is the wrong understanding of emptiness. That is why Śākyamuni Buddha emphasized, "You should not doubt this. Form is emptiness. Conversely, emptiness is form."

Through examining worldly phenomena through dependent origination, you can see that even substantial forms of matter are illusory and empty. But even though they are illusions, when the proper causes and conditions have come together, they exist. "Emptiness is form" means that illusory phenomena are not different from each other.

With regards to matter, the Buddha said that, "Form is not different from emptiness. Emptiness is not different from form." Ordinary people cannot let go of distinguishing between different types of matter because of their habits. It is difficult for such people to see the empty nature of material things. But this is the truth of the universe. That is why the *Heart Sutra* repeats again, "Form is emptiness. Emptiness is form."

7. The Same Is True of Feeling, Perception, Mental formations, and Consciousness

Everything is subject to dependent origination. All things must have favorable conditions to arise. If you base your thoughts upon this, you will come to know that the mental aggregates of feeling, perception, mental formations, and consciousness are all empty. Feeling includes sorrow, joy, pain, pleasure, and equanimity. Don't all of these feelings rely on causes and conditions?

How many causes and conditions are necessary to see the object in front of you? Many. First, there needs to be space between you and the object. There must be light, and the object must be in your line of vision. After your eyes have perceived an object, a visual-mental process (eye consciousness) carries the information to your mind consciousness. The mind consciousness then deems the object attractive or unattractive. See how it takes so many causes and conditions to see something attractive? Because this feeling arises from causes and conditions, once these causes and conditions change the feeling will cease. Thus feelings do not truly exist, they are empty just like everything else. "Feeling is not different from emptiness. Emptiness is not different from feeling."

Right now, you are forming perceptions. Does perception require causes and conditions? Perhaps you would reply, "We aren't looking or listening. We're only perceiving and thinking." Perhaps you assume that thinking does not require causes and conditions. After all, it's not as if you're using your eyes when you think. But what is it that your mind is engaged in during perception? Your *ālaya* consciousness has stored impressions accumulated through many lifetimes, not just memories of your current life. These are the conditions for you to think so much.

For instance, consider this thought: "Although I am not currently in Ladakh, India, it's a really beautiful region. I'd like to go back there next year." When you think this, your eyes and ears do not see or hear the scenery of Ladakh, but because you have been there before, your mind contains impressions from your experiences there. When you remember such things, they become mental causes. Thus, perception too relies upon causes and conditions, and as such lacks self-nature. "Perception is not different from emptiness. Emptiness is not different from perception."

Mental formations are the thoughts we use to make decisions. When you decide, "Should I go or not?" several kinds of thoughts will arise. Such mental formations are also subject to dependent origination. As time passes, they change. For example, if I said, "If you two are going to Ladakh, then I'll go too", you may say, "I'll give you ten thousand dollars not to go. How's that sound?" "Fine. Then I won't go." Mental formations are impermanent and change with time and other variables. "Mental formations are not different from emptiness. Emptiness is not different from mental formations."

8. The Origin of Consciousness from the Twelve Links of Dependent Origination

The aggregate of consciousness refers to the mind consciousness, as well as the *manas* consciousness and the *ālaya* consciousness. These can be considered the primary centers of mental function. The link of "mental formations" in the twelve links of dependent origination refers to our physical, verbal, and mental behavior from previous lives. The next link, "consciousness" refers specifically to the *ālaya* consciousness, which stores the impressions of behavior from previous lifetimes.

The link "name and form" refers to the material and the mental, body and mind. It arises and functions together with the *ālaya* consciousness. Do not think of them as arising in sequence. The primary function of name and form is to make "contact" with sense objects and give rise to "feeling." Through this process, "craving," "clinging," and "becoming" arise.

"Craving" is a mental effect. "Craving" is thinking endlessly about favorable, attractive sense objects, or your own favorite people, events, things, and other such phenomena. "Clinging" is a physical action. Whether it is a bodily or verbal action, both create seeds that are stored in the *ālaya* consciousness. This process is called "becoming." When this life comes to an end, the force of "becoming" is what gives rise to "consciousness" in the next life.

The twelve links of dependent origination don't need to be too complicated, and it is not necessary to explain each one in detail. Understanding "craving" and "clinging" is enough. The primary functions of human life revolve around "craving" and "clinging." The impressions left by "craving" and "clinging" mix to form the *ālaya* consciousness. Even as our actions fade away each day, memories of those actions are left behind in the *ālaya* consciousness. When we enter our next life, they form the basis of our next existence.

What are "craving" and "clinging" made of? It can be describes in a single word: "ignorance." Craving and clinging are the product of improper attachment, the result of an ignorant conception of the self. Ignorance comes from mistaking the self to be real. We believe in the self and have a view of the self. Because we affirm the self, we cling to the self and become self-centered. We feel that we are better than others, and deserve preferential treatment. We are ignorant of the self, have views of the self, take pride in the self, and crave the self.

The cycle of birth and death is maintained by ignorance. "Ignorance" is incorrect thinking. "Craving" and "clinging" are incorrect behavior. These behaviors manifest as "becoming." "Becoming" arises from past "ignorance" and "mental formations." All three of these links act as conditions upon the "consciousness" of the next life. "Mental formations," the collection of past physical, verbal, and mental actions, lead to the present physical, verbal, and mental actions of "craving" and "clinging." All "craving" is a product of ignorance, and lead us to seek, pursue, and desire. These become sentiment and affection, which is why another name for living beings in Chinese is *youqing* (有情), "with sentiment."

The sutras describe sentient beings as "covered by ignorance and bound by the shackles of craving." The first part refers to being covered by the ignorance of incorrect thought. When this happens, pure wisdom cannot manifest. The following phrase depicts craving as akin to being shackled. Once a person craves something, even if they are told they cannot have it, they will be drawn to it regardless. They will act first and think later. The result is suffering. It is too late for regrets. That is why craving is like being shackled. This is how we currently live. This is the nature of birth and death.

The aggregate of consciousness includes the six sense consciousnesses, as discussed previously. It also includes all our stored behaviors from many previous lives. The mind can be stirred to reveal traces of previous existences. This is the *ālaya* consciousness, though more generally we may call it "mind," "thought," or "consciousness."

The *ālaya* consciousness is not independent. It is like a storehouse full of thoughts and actions which pile up day by day. It too arises through causes and conditions. Mind, thought, and consciousness do not have a physical form. They are described by the *Heart Sutra* as "Form is not different from emptiness, emptiness is not different from form. Form is emptiness. Emptiness is form."

The *ālaya* consciousness is difficult to understand. Let's talk about physics for a moment. What makes a light bulb shine? What are the causes? The light bulb shines because a power plant generates electricity for it. This electricity is composed of countless millions of electrons. One electron follows another to light the bulb. Ultimately, would we say they are acting individually, or together?

If we use a state-of-the-art, high-tech microscope, we can see that there is space between all of the electrons. Scientists have long known about the structure of atoms, made up of electrons, protons, and neutrons. From atomic structure diagrams, we can see how positive and negative electrical charges attract one another. Such images are magnified many thousands of times for us to see them.

Electricity is continually generated and distributed from power plants. This electricity comes from tightly packed groups of countless electrons. These electrons appear to have no space between them, however, even though the electrons are packed together tightly, there are still small gaps between them. Can you believe that? If that was not the case, then once you turned on a light bulb it would stay lit forever. Rays of light would be fixed inside the bulb. How does an electrical meter tick? They work because there is space between electrons. That is why there needs to be a constant power source.

Within the Buddhist understanding of causes and conditions, there exists the principle of "uninterrupted concurrent conditions," which means that cause and conditions have almost no gaps between them. When power plants supply energy, the space between electrons is so minute that it is virtually non-existent. The *ālaya* consciousness also has small gaps. As one thought ceases the next follows so closely that it is almost as if there were no gaps whatsoever.

Consciousness is empty. It arises depending on causes and conditions. It is the accumulation of the impressions left behind from behaviors from all our previous lives. "Consciousness is not different from emptiness. Emptiness is not different from consciousness. Consciousness is emptiness, emptiness is consciousness." This can be derived from the *Heart Sutra*, when it says that "The same is true of feeling, perception, mental formations, and consciousness." This shows that feeling, perception, mental formations, and consciousness all have the same relationship to emptiness that form does. Physical phenomena are empty. Mental phenomena are also empty. Both are empty. One could simply say that the five aggregates are all empty.

9. All Phenomena Are Empty. They Do Not Arise or Cease, Are Not Defiled or Pure, Do Not Increase or Decrease.

The *Diamond Sutra* mentions five different sets of "eyes" we can possess: eyes of flesh, heavenly eyes, wisdom eyes, Dharma eyes, and Buddha eyes. Examine the world with *prajñā*-wisdom and you will see the emptiness within it. This is the wisdom of dependent origination, and this perspective is called "wisdom eyes." What is there to gain from this teaching? In the *Heart Sutra*, Sariputra is told to "contemplate deeply the *prajñāparamita*," which means to continuously rely upon this teaching.

Mahāyāna bodhisattvas are the product of the deep realization of such thought. They can see how "Mountains are not mountains, and water is not water." The illusions of the mundane world disappear from their minds.

For example, suppose you are in class and, suddenly, you think of your hometown. "I wonder what mom is doing? I'm not even sure what's going on over there these days. There used to be a little kid I'd bump into back in the day. I wonder how old he is now?" Though you may still be sitting in class, your mind is absorbed in nostalgia and remembrance. The world in front of you vanishes, and all that remains is the realm within the mind.

I also often use this example: Suppose you are in the middle of reading, when you suddenly think about your hometown. Though your eyes are still focused on the book, your mind is thinking about people and things from back home. To you, it is as though the book has disappeared. Your mind is now focused entirely on life at home.

Similarly, when we examine the world with *prajñā*-wisdom, our mind is focused entirely on emptiness and the perfect tranquility of *nirvāṇa*. External sense objects disappear and the true nature of emptiness manifests. Form drops away, and the nature of things become known. What can we learn from this? All phenomena do not arise or cease, are not defiled or pure, and do not increase or decrease. The formation, arising, cessation, quality, disposition, and quantity of all people, events, and things within the world are affected by causes and conditions. After they arise they cannot remain constant and unchanging. Such things are illusions, they are not real. They are false and empty.

The *Heart Sutra* says, "All phenomena are empty. They do not arise or cease, are not defiled or pure, do not increase or decrease." Buddhist practitioners should use *prajñā*-wisdom to view all things. They should enter meditative concentration, submerging the mind in the wisdom of emptiness. All things do not arise or cease, are not defiled or pure, and do not increase or decrease. In this way, entering *nirvāṇa* becomes possible. "*Nirvāṇa*" means no arising and no ceasing, no defilement and no purity, no increasing and no decreasing, and no coming or going.

10. No Eye, Ear, Nose, Tongue, Body, or Mind

When we enter *nirvāṇa*, external forms disappear. That is why it is said that, "in emptiness, there is no form." When all is seen as empty in nature, then there is no attachment to the discriminations of the phenomenal world. This is the state in which bodhisattvas are said to "See that mountains are not mountains, and that water is not water." The sutras say that, "*Prajñā* is like a great fire. All things that are close to it will be burned. What touches it will be harmed." Why is *prajñā* said to be like a great fire? The "fire" spoken of here is a metaphor for wisdom. The flames of a fire can burn all material things into ash. Profound wisdom can destroy all kinds of defilement. When all conditioned phenomena come in contact with *prajñā*-wisdom, all their marks and characteristics vanish from the minds of bodhisattvas, leaving behind their empty nature. "In Emptiness, there is no form." Instead, it can be said that "while contemplating deeply the *prajñāparamita*," the wisdom eyes of bodhisattvas see that there is nothing to be seen.

By understanding everything is of empty nature, we see that everything is made of false forms. The *Diamond Sutra* says "All forms are illusory." When this is realized, your practice of stopping and seeing meditation will become a habit, transforming your outlook on life. This is how you can use your wisdom eyes in daily life.

The *Heart Sutra* declares that there is "No eye, ear, nose, tongue, body, or mind." The body makes use of sense organs to perceive the outside world, including the eyes, ears, nose, and tongue. The body itself is considered a sense organ, and if we include the mind we have six sense organs in total. In Chinese, the six sense organs are referred to figuratively with the character *gen* (根), "root," because these "roots" can grow into discrimination and defilement. The eyes, ears, nose, and tongue are included within the organ of the body, though they each have their own function. The eyes respond to light and color, the ears to various sounds, the nose to various aromas, and the tongue responds to flavors such as sweet, sour, bitter, and spicy. The sense organs can be divided in this way.

Everyone should know which stimuli in their daily lives are the most likely to trigger illusory thoughts. In Japan, there is a Shinto shrine called Nikkō Tōshō-gū that is famous for its carving of three monkeys. One monkey is covering its ears, one is covering its eyes, and the third monkey is covering its mouth. It warns us to be cautious of what we speak, listen to, and look upon. These are highlighted because the eyes, ears, and mouth are the most common triggers of illusory thoughts.

After we understand that "in emptiness, there are no forms," we will know to turn inward when we make contact with external sense objects. In this way we will see that our eyes do not have eye nature, our ears do not have ear nature, and our nose does not have nose nature. All things are illusory formations constructed from causes and conditions. When those causes and conditions come apart, the illusions they formed will cease as well. When we are born, we are not given true eyes or a true nose. When we die, we return to formlessness, still lacking true eyes, ears, and noses. Consequently, in the quote "No eye, ear, nose, tongue, body, or mind," the word "no" means that these sense organs lack self-nature.

11. No Form, Sound, Smell, Taste, Touch or Dharmas

Earlier in the *Heart Sutra*, the paragraph beginning with "Sariputra, all phenomena are empty," is followed by a method of analysis, culminating in "in emptiness, there are no forms." We should view the world in this way. For example, suppose we apply this view to ourselves. We can see that our own "form, feeling, perception, mental formations, and consciousness" lack self-nature. We can see how our sense organs of "eyes, ears, nose, tongue, body, and mind" also lack self-nature. Considering external sense objects, "form, sound, smell, taste, and touch" lack self-nature as well. Without this and without that, we can see that the external world as well as the body and mind are empty.

"Form, sound, smell, taste, and touch" make contact with the "eyes, ears, nose, tongue, and body" in order to perceive external phenomena and separate them into various categories. The reason we have the five desires for the external world is that we do not see these various forms, sounds, smells, tastes, and touches as all subject to dependent origination and lacking self-nature. We become attached blindly and pursue our desires.

For example, suppose two objects strike each other and create a sound. By the time you hear the sound, the sound waves have already traveled through space and have dissipated without a trace. Sound is subject to dependent origination and lacks self-nature. In the same way, taste arises when the tongue is distinguishing between foods. After food passes the tongue and is swallowed, the sensation of taste quickly passes. Taste is also subject to dependent origination and lacks self-nature. All matter, regardless of its shape or appearance, is continually deteriorating, aging, and losing its former luster. Even if it is happening too slowly for us to see, this deterioration is still present. The external sense objects of forms, sounds, smells, tastes, and touch continuously change in accordance with dependent origination. They have no self-nature.

To prevent external sense objects from giving rise to illusory thoughts and desires, one must guard the sense organs, eat and drink in moderation, be dedicated to wakefulness, and have a mind that is content and detached. "Guarding the sense organs" means to take good care of your ears, eyes, nose, tongue, body, and mind. Keep your sense organs from overstimulation through frivolous sights, sounds, and speech. Uphold the precepts in your daily life. To put it another way, uphold right speech, right action, and right livelihood from the Noble Eightfold Path.

It is especially important to be content with what you do not have. For example, when you see people who have fancy new electronics, you should not envy them. If you do not have envy, you will not be troubled. Besides, there is already plenty that is available to you—it would take you more time than you have left in your life to read all the books in the library. What does it mean to have a mind that is detached? A detached mind is one that does not envy the good fortune or merit of others. For example, suppose you are living in a Buddhist seminary, and you discover some of your classmates are going to study abroad in Hong Kong, you should just think to yourself, "It's better to stay at the Buddhist seminary anyways. Staying here is more practical. Besides, running around as a traveler is exhausting."

The mind should be detached. In this way, we will not desire external sense objects, and can make progress in cultivating meditative concentration. As we become adept at meditative concentration, we should continue to abide with right wisdom. "Right wisdom," in this instance means realizing when your mind has strayed from your meditation object, and immediately re-establishing focus. Being dedicated to wakefulness can be used as another way to cultivate meditative concentration, in which the practitioner visualizes a bright light before sleep. Imagine that before your eyes there is a radiant disk of light. Slowly, your mind will become clear even as you sleep.

As practitioners develop the power of meditative concentration, they will become aware of thoughts at the moment they arise, and can determine if they are pure or impure. Are these strings of thought wholesome or unwholesome in nature? Should these actions be undertaken or not? Should these words be spoken or not? Should we go somewhere or not? When the mind stirs and thoughts arise, they should be clearly understood. Only in this way can the four right efforts be practiced.

The "four right efforts" are to strengthen wholesome mental states that are present, develop wholesome mental states that are not yet present, end unwholesome mental states that are present, and prevent unwholesome mental states from arising that are not yet present. In summation, they are to cultivate what is wholesome and put an end to what is unwholesome. Often, the allure of external sense objects can be too tempting to resist. At those times, we may have unwholesome, immoral thoughts. But we should not allow these thoughts to continue to arise or multiply.

Even if you are aware that you should not look at unwholesome things, you may find you still want to steal a peek. This means that your powers of meditative concentration are insufficient. Without the power of meditative concentration, you will have no means with which to control your thoughts. With the power of meditative concentration, you will be able to prevent yourself from looking at unwholesome things, cutting off your desire immediately. This will prevent unwholesome behavior, and you will not have to suffer future negative karmic effects.

Without the power of meditative concentration, the four right efforts cannot be cultivated. In addition to upholding precepts, we should diligently cultivate meditative concentration and the four right efforts. In this way, we can examine the phenomena of daily life according to the Dharma, and achieve the state of "No eye, ear, nose, tongue, body, or mind; no form, sound, smell, taste, touch or *dharmas*."

12. No Eye Consciousness So on unto Mind Consciousness

When the six sense organs of the body, the six sense objects of the outside world, and the six sense consciousnesses of the mind are taken together they are called *shiba jie* (十八界), "eighteen realms." In this context, "realm" means "category" or "scope." The eyes, ears, nose, tongue, body, and mind each have different functions, which make contact with the six sense objects and give rise to the six sense consciousnesses. All eighteen are different.

The eyes distinguish material things by their visual qualities, such as length, shape, size, and colors such as blue, yellow, red, and white. This process of distinction gives rise to eye consciousness. The ears distinguish positive and negative sounds, and give rise to ear consciousness. Nose consciousness arises from the nose distinguishing fragrant and putrid smells. The tongue distinguishes flavors such as sour, bitter, and spicy, giving rise to tongue consciousness. Body consciousness arises from the body distinguishing between tactile sensations such as hot or cold, hard or soft, coarse or fine, and rough or smooth. The mind distinguishes between thoughts, giving rise to mind consciousness.

As can be seen above, the six sense organs must make contact with their corresponding sense objects in order for the six sense consciousnesses to arise. These three arise at the same time, they cannot be separated chronologically. Consequently, the six sense consciousnesses cannot exist independently. They are subject to dependent origination and lack self-nature. This is the meaning of "No eye consciousness so on unto mind consciousness" If you understand that the six sense consciousnesses are empty, you can cure yourself of an arrogant, selfish mind.

People often become arrogant when they believe they are more dignified, healthier, smarter, or wealthier than others. An ordinary person only needs to be a little bit better or a little bit more able than others before arrogance begins to arise.

For instance, suppose a co-worker of yours is promoted to supervisor. Before when the two of you were peers, everything was fine. But now your former co-worker addresses you differently. Arrogance arises very easily. In daily life, it is important to remember

"No eye consciousness so on unto mind consciousness" to alleviate arrogance.

The *Heart Sutra* is about human life. It is not only to be read during ceremonies for those who have passed away. During such services, after the main chanting has been completed, but before the altar is approached and the merit of the ceremony is dedicated to liberate the deceased, an homage to Cooling Ground Bodhisattva is recited (Nāmó qīngliángdì púsà). Afterward, the *Heart Sutra* is chanted once, followed by a recitation of the "Short Prayer for Rebirth in the Western Pure Land." During this time the presiding monastic uses the contemplations on the *Heart Sutra* described above to urge the deceased to let go of their attachments and aspire to rebirth in the Western Pure Land of Ultimate Bliss, so they can be liberated from birth and death.

If you chant the *Heart Sutra* each day, you will come to see that the five aggregates are all empty. That way, you will be able to leave confusion and delusion behind and be without fear. Contemplate in this way and you will be at ease.

13. No Ignorance and Extinction of Ignorance

The first link of the twelve links of dependent origination is "ignorance." In this instance, "ignorance" refers to not knowing the true form of the world. Ignorance causes greed, anger, and delusion to arise, which inhibit wisdom and prevent us from attaining liberation. How much bitterness did the Buddha taste? How much suffering did he endure while cultivating ascetic practices? Only by experiencing innumerable hardships was he able to attain enlightenment. After attaining enlightenment, he explained, "all phenomena arise from causes and conditions, and they cease from causes and conditions." Nothing in this world manifests on its own. Everything depends on causes and conditions.

Put in this way, the truth of the universe seems easy to understand. As such, we may question its importance. However, these two phrases were enough for Śāriputra to enter the first stage of arhatship. The Buddha employed skillful means and excellent technique to teach us, but sentient beings were still doubtful. "Is enlightenment that simple? Is it as simple as that?" It really is that simple. After attaining enlightenment, you will have limitless reverence and respect for the Buddha.

There is a saying that, "A room that has been dark for one thousand years can be instantly illuminated with a single light." Since beginningless time, we have always thought about our "self." This ignorance needs to be removed by contemplating *prajñā*-wisdom, right view from the Noble Eightfold Path, and the three Dharma seals. After examination and contemplation, you will be able to confirm that nothing within this world is fixed or unchanging. There are no people, events, or objects that exist independently. In this way, all of our past attachments to ignorance about the self, views of the self, pride in the self, and craving for the self will be severed. Saying something "lacks true reality" does not only refer to external sense objects. Even one's own self lacks true reality. The main point of the *Heart Sutra* is that self is not real. When attachment to self is removed, you will be enlightened.

"Enlightenment" and "ignorance" are also unreal. For example, a room can be lit up at night with the simple flick of a switch, but with another flip the room can turn pitch black. Where did that darkness run off to? When we turn off the lights, the brightness goes away. So, which window did the light jump out of? The nature of ignorance is empty. How then can there truly be a thing called "ignorance"?

In Chinese, ignorance is expressed with the two characters *wuming* (無明), "lacking brightness." *Ming* (明), "brightness" or "light" is another way to say wisdom. Once we become wise, has our ignorance gone away? No! It has only changed form. In Buddhism we say that "affliction is *bodhi*," which is another way of saying that there truly is no ignorance. We can't take this thing called "ignorance" and separate it from the mind, tossing it out. That is why the *Heart Sutra* says "no ignorance and extinction of ignorance."

Think this through and you will no longer be confused. Your past misconceptions will be gone. Once you assumed that everything truly existed unto itself. Now you know that everything in the world, whatever it happens to be, arose through causes and conditions.

The *Heart Sutra* continues, "no aging and death and no extinction of aging and death." Without birth, how can there be old age and death? Old age and death also arise through causes and conditions. They are not real. After bodhisattvas see that "old age and death" are not real, they will know that at this very moment the cycle of birth and death is *nirvāṇa*, and that affliction is *bodhi*.

When it comes to life, the *Heart Sutra* chiefly addresses self-liberation and self-awakening. The latter half of the *Heart Sutra* says, "Bodhisattvas who rely on the *prajñāparamita* ... will ultimately reach *nirvāṇa*." Bodhisattvas contemplate the emptiness of all phenomena, but first and foremost they contemplate the emptiness of the self. Only by understanding the emptiness of the self can we remove the notion of a self. Only then can we follow the bodhisattva path and attain Buddhahood.

14. No Suffering, Cause of Suffering, Cessation, or Path

Suffering is also an illusory phenomena. The suffering of birth, old age, sickness, and death as well as the suffering of separation from loved ones, closeness to loathsome people, and not getting what we want are all the product of impressions from craving and clinging from previous lives. In previous lives, we may have acted in ways that are positive or negative, envious or generous, and wholesome or unwholesome. These impressions are recorded and stored in the *ālaya* consciousness.

When we are reborn, the impressions stored in our *ālaya* consciousness reach fruition and manifest throughout our lives. Sometimes this creates beneficial causes and conditions, while at other times the causes and conditions produced can be disastrous. Perhaps one may have followed other religions, but now causes and conditions have come together to lead you to Buddhism. This is an effect of causes and conditions from previous lives.

The many impressions we accumulate over our lifetimes reflect our experiences in the world. At times, they manifest themselves as moments of happiness or suffering. But this "suffering" should not be taken as real in the least. Like all phenomena, suffering arises from causes and conditions. Kṣitigarbha Bodhisattva resides in hell alongside other sentient beings. Because of the content of their consciousness, sentient beings in hell feel great suffering. On the other hand, Kṣitigarbha Bodhisattva did not arrive in hell because of negative causes, and thus he does not suffer there.

What is the cause of suffering? Under the influence of past ignorance, craving and clinging has ceaselessly generated physical,

Ksitigarbha Bodhisattva

Ksitigarbha Bodhisattva is venerated throughout the Buddhist world, and is also known as the "bodhisattva of great vows," because he vowed to go to the hell realm to teach and liberate the sentient beings who reside there. Specifically, Ksitigarbha vowed to delay his own enlightenment until the hell realms are vacant, with the words: "Not until hell is vacant shall I become a Buddha; only when all sentient beings are liberated will I attain *bodhi*."

verbal, and mental actions. These actions combine and become the force that pushes us towards further rebirth. In this way, the cause of suffering also arises through causes and conditions, and in that sense, is not real.

What is the cessation of suffering? It is how the Buddha taught us to end our afflictions. This doesn't mean that our afflictions are destroyed as if they are some kind of object, but they are removed through understanding emptiness. Though it can be said that bodhisattvas truly enter *nirvāṇa*, they are still without attainment. This is difficult for ordinary people to comprehend. This is especially true of Chinese Buddhists, most of whom follow the Pure Land School, the Chan School, or the Esoteric School. It is a pity that such a profound teaching is hard for them to experience.

What is the path? It is one's method of spiritual cultivation. The Noble Eightfold Path is the means the Buddha taught us to directly experience the truth. But what path do we follow after we attain enlightenment? In the *Diamond Sutra*, the Buddha says, "Even my teachings should be understood to be like a raft. If even the Dharma must be let go of, what about what is not the Dharma?"

For example, someone may use a boat to ferry across a stream, but the boat is just a tool. Once the other shore has been reached, it would be impractical to bring the boat with you! The path is also just a tool, it is not a truly existing phenomena.

15. No Wisdom and No Attainment

"No wisdom and no attainment," does not literally mean that wisdom does not exist and there is nothing to be gained. It means that wisdom is also empty of self-nature when examined from the perspective of dependent origination. This is called "wisdom beyond differentiation." Even the wisdom of true enlightenment is empty, just as the external sense objects of form, sound, smell, taste, touch, and *dharmas* are empty. Wisdom beyond differentiation can be used to examine sense objects without differentiation and distinguishing and see that all is empty. This is what is meant by "no wisdom and no attainment."

The next part of the *Heart Sutra*, beginning with "As there is no attainment..." is a summary of the previous paragraph. Why is there "No eye, ear, nose, tongue, body, or mind; no form, sound, smell, taste, touch or *dharmas*; no eye consciousness so on unto mind consciousness; no ignorance and extinction of ignorance; even unto no aging and death and no extinction of aging and death; no suffering, cause of suffering, cessation, or path; no wisdom and no attainment"? Because they are all empty!

The *Diamond Sutra* mentions giving rise to a mind that does not abide in anything. This means using the empty-natured wisdom of "no attainment" as a foundation to liberate all sentient beings. This is necessary for bodhisattvas to practice the six perfections and be utterly without fear. They do not fear the long-term commitment of attaining Buddhahood. They are confident that even difficult tasks can be completed. They will endure what is hard to endure. In this way they are at ease. As the *Heart Sutra* says, "All the Buddhas of the past, present, and future rely on the *prajñāparamita* to attain *anuttara-samyak-sambodhi*." *Anuttara-samyak-sambodhi* is the highest form of enlightenment, and as the sutra says, it is attained through *prajñā!* If we can manage our affairs in the same way, we will have great freedom.

Inner Transcendence

Even if we realize that the five aggregates are empty, there is still an illusory "self" formed by the five illusory aggregates. But if we can see that this "self" is empty, we can remove our attachment to this illusion. Again, this can be compared to reading a book. The book is right in front of your face, but when illusory thoughts arise your mind is in that faraway place. Your eyes may be looking at the page, but you don't understand the words in front of you.

In the same way, we can continue to deepen our wisdom through *huatou* practice using passages from the sutras like, "all phenomena are illusory," or "all conditioned phenomena are like dreams, illusions, bubbles, and shadows," while keeping in mind the empty nature of dependent origination and that form is not different from emptiness, and emptiness is not different from form. As our power of concentration deepens, we enter a state in which there is nothing to be attained and nothing to be seen. This is inner transcendence.

Though the mind can be wiped of illusory external sense objects, these sense objects do not simply disappear. It is like when you are reading a book, but your mind is elsewhere. You know that all phenomena are illusory and you can see through them to the true form of reality. When the mind can abide in this way, you can see that phenomena do not arise or cease, are not defiled or pure, and do not increase or decrease. That is why bodhisattvas are able to liberate sentient beings without obstruction: they know that all phenomena are illusory.

This is how to apply the *Heart Sutra* in your daily practice. After realizing and understanding these truths, you can see the emptiness of sense objects as they arise. Work diligently and skillfully at this every day and you can be liberated and at ease. This is Humanistic Buddhism: the Buddhism of daily life.

Living at Ease

In the Chan School there is a saying, "You are a Buddha." You should ask yourself, "What is a Buddha?" To answer that question, you must be able to experience all things including this present moment just as they are. You will understand Chan poems, such as

"Lush green bamboo are wondrous truths; luxuriant yellow flowers are nothing but *prajñā*-wisdom," and "The sounds of the rippling
creek are all words of the Buddha. The mountain scene is none other
than the body of the Dharma." Everything lacks self-nature. This is
the present moment just as it is.

If you truly understand, you can live at ease. You will have the
serenity of a bodhisattva, constantly wearing a benevolent smile.
Buddhas and bodhisattvas do not always appear solemn and sa-
gacious, but are also capable of kindness, such as when the Buddha is depicted with a gentle smile. Their minds are utterly clear.
Practitioners who uphold the precepts will also gain a dignified
appearance and a compassionate disposition. They will no longer
be burdened by resentment or dissatisfaction. They will embody
kindness and their minds will gain profound wisdom. With utter
mental clarity, all obstacles are removed. They spend their lives
happy, unburdened by worry and anxiety. They see that the five
aggregates are all empty.

Emptiness and the Six Perfections

To uphold the precepts, we should not think of ourselves as "pre-
cept holders." Nor should we consider the notion of violating the
precepts. "Upholding precepts" cannot be attained, just as merit from
upholding precepts cannot be attained. To cultivate patience, we
must let go of the notion of "self," just as we must let go of the notion of "others." Without self or others, what is there to be impatient
about? Patience too lacks self-nature.

Once one sees all phenomena and the self as empty, this can complete the practice of the first five perfections. Giving, patience, morality, diligence, and meditative concentration all also lack self-nature. When cultivating these perfections, you should do so without
the notion of a self. One should give and be patient with no notion

of others who receive. The five aggregates of the self are empty, as are the five aggregates of others.

It is under these circumstances that sentient beings, dreamlike and illusory, are liberated, and one arrives at the state of "non-abiding." With the mind no longer attached to anything, one is said to be "detached from all phenomena," and without any notion of self, others, or sentient beings. There is no coming or going, arising or ceasing, or birth and death. In the *Diamond Sutra* this is called "no notion of longevity." Leaving these four notions behind, cutting off all doubt, and abiding in nothing, this is the practice of a bodhisattva.

Bodhisattvas should not abide in anything. They should not abide in form, sound, smell, taste, or *dharmas*. They should practice giving, morality, patience, diligence, and meditative concentration. All of these are lead by *prajñā*-wisdom. By practicing the six perfections in everything they do, bodhisattvas abide in nothing, leaving behind all notions. By living in this way they are bodhisattvas. If they had any abiding, they would not be called bodhisattvas.

A Life of Liberation

Some eminent, enlightened monastics, such as Venerable Jìgōng and Venerable Bùdài, had wild, jovial appearances. Such people have seen through the things of the world. This world is covered in illusion, and if you see through it, you will no longer care about wealth, power, or rank. Perhaps you might say, "Well, what if my boss gave me the axe tomorrow? I wouldn't even know where my next meal would come from. Could I still smile at a time like that?" Indeed, lay Buddhists are more subject to obstacles arising from causes and conditions. It is more difficult for them to cultivate the path.

But if you know and follow the teachings of the *Heart Sutra*, then even if you wind up penniless, you will know that all things arise from causes and conditions. Poverty arises from the causes and conditions of poverty, just as wealth arises from the causes and conditions of wealth. Nothing can get in the way of this. All it takes is a compassionate heart, right wisdom and right view, and the willingness to give rise to the bodhi mind. If all of these are present, there is always a way. You may be poor, but will not starve to death. Only in this way can you live free and at ease and avoid obstruction.

Past attachment and greed are what the *Heart Sutra* call "confusion and delusion." By seeing the five aggregates as empty, you can avoid misconceptions like "this is mine and that is yours," and "I like this, but I hate that." By thinking in this way, you can take life as it comes and leave confusion and delusion far behind.

If the conditions exist, and something is about to happen, then it will happen. If the right conditions do not exist, and it is not imminent, then it won't happen, and it is best to let it go. Following causes and conditions allows a person to be at ease. This is the only way to be free and at ease and attain liberation! There is no teaching higher than this. It is profound, accords with the Middle Way, and can remove all suffering. This is the truth. It is a rare occurrence to hear such a teaching. Even if you are poor in this life, if you live and practice in accordance with the Buddha's teachings, you can be free. The first part of the *Heart Sutra*'s Sanskrit Mantra is "*gate gate*," which brings benefit to those who read it. The mantra means, "Go forth, go forth! Take refuge in the Triple Gem. Together we will take refuge in you!" The *Heart Sutra* is excerpted from the much larger *Mahaprajñāpāramitā Sutra*. It's very short, functioning as a summary of what practitioners can use in their cultivation. The *Heart Sutra* is not recited for the sake of the Buddha, it is a guide for all of us to practice.

Chapter Eleven

BODHISATTVA PRACTICE

Reading the Diamond Sutra

The *Diamond Sutra* and the *Heart Sutra* vary in their empha-sis. The *Heart Sutra* places greater emphasis on self-liberation, whereas the *Diamond Sutra* takes the next step and describes how Mahāyāna bodhisattvas use the wisdom gained from their own liberation to liberate other sentient beings. In this way, the *Diamond Sutra* can be read as a treatise on the practice of a bodhisattva. It is the earliest sutra to receive mass dissemination in China, and is also one of the one most popular and common Buddhist sutras.

The sutra opens with a description of the Buddha's lifestyle and goes on to explain the reason why the sutra was spoken. Beginning with, "Thus have I heard. At one time, the Buddha was in the city of Sravasti at the Jeta Grove Monastery..." to "When he had finished eating, he put away his robe and bowl, washed his feet, straightened his mat, and sat down." This preface explains the causes and conditions from which Śākyamuni Buddha came to teach the contents of the sutra.

The focus of the second chapter is the Buddha's clarification of Subhūti's question. In response, the Buddha says, "The Tathāgata protects and is concerned about all bodhisattvas, and instructs all bodhisattvas." This means that the Tathāgata is able to use great technique and skillful means to guide bodhisattvas to cultivate the seeds of Buddhahood, emulate the Buddha's wisdom, and ensure that the Mahāyāna teachings are passed on to future generations. The focus of the *Diamond Sutra* are the vows, wisdom, and practices of bodhisattvas and the methods they use to liberate sentient beings.

The Bodhi Mind in the Diamond Sutra

The *Diamond Sutra* calls upon practitioners to give rise to the *bodhi* mind. *Bodhi* is a Sanskrit word which means "enlightened wisdom." The wisdom of arhats, pratyekabuddhas, and Buddhas are all called *bodhi*. Within those three types of wisdom, the Buddha's wisdom is the greatest and most perfect. It is called, *anuttara samyaksambodhi*, which means "unsurpassed perfect enlightenment." Practitioners who wish to attain the *bodhi* of a Buddha must vow to cultivate the bodhisattva path and liberate sentient beings. After making this vow and practicing for three great *kalpas* will they become Buddhas. The *Diamond Sutra* describes those who give rise to the mind to attain *anuttara samyaksambodhi* as not afraid of the hardships of liberating sentient beings nor the vast length of the Buddhist path. They are able to maintain their intention to liberate sentient beings. To ensure that they do not regress, bodhisattvas diligently develop the wisdom of emptiness, so that they can liberate sentient beings without regressing. This is a unique quality of the *Diamond Sutra*: the combination of the concept of the *bodhi* mind and the wisdom of emptiness.

Mundane Bodhi Mind and Supreme Bodhi Mind

There are two types of *bodhi* mind: the mundane *bodhi* mind and the supreme *bodhi* mind. The mundane *bodhi* mind is the intention generated by a bodhisattva who is still an ordinary person. From taking the five precepts or the bodhisattva precepts, you can give rise to the *bodhi* mind and hope to become a Buddha. After this initial intention, bodhisattvas hear and think about the Buddha's teachings and they diligently practice meditative concentration.

Gradually such people learn the truth of the universe, all phenomena, and of emptiness. After they realize emptiness through meditative concentration, they become arhats. Then the supreme *bodhi* mind arises: instead of entering the liberation of the *arhat*, they re-enter the cycle of birth and death. In every life thereafter, they work to liberate sentient beings. This is the emphasis of the *Diamond Sutra*: how the bodhisattvas use the supreme *bodhi* mind to cultivate the bodhisattva path.

Leading All Sentient Beings to Nirvāna

In the *Diamond Sutra* the first teaching given by Śākyamuni Buddha to the bodhisattvas is an answer to the question, "What should we abide in? How do we subdue our minds?" Whether bodhisattvas have the mundane *bodhi* mind or the supreme *bodhi* mind, both wish to help all sentient beings enter final *nirvāṇa*.

To answer the question, the Buddha divides "all sentient beings" into a number of categories:

> Of all sentient beings, be they born of eggs, wombs, moisture, or transformation, or whether they have form, or no form, or whether they are able to perceive, or do not perceive, or are neither able to perceive nor not perceive.

The categories above are known as the "four forms of birth" and the "nine realms of existence." The "four forms of birth" refer to the method of birth, dividing sentient beings into those born from eggs, from wombs, from moisture, and through transformation. The "nine realms of existence" refer to various states of meditative concentration. The first of the nine realms includes the many possible places of rebirth throughout the desire realm, including the hell realm, hungry ghost realm, animal realm, *asura* realm, human realm, and heavenly realm. The second through the fifth realms as a group are the form realms, and correspond to the first, second, third, and fourth *dhyānas*. The sixth through ninth realm describe formless realms, including the realm of limitless space, the realm of limitless consciousness, the realm of nothingness, and the realm of neither thought nor non-thought.

Within these nine realms of existence, beings can be separated into those with and without physical bodies ("form, or no form"), and various levels of meditative concentration ("able to perceive, or do not perceive, or are neither able to perceive nor not perceive") But no matter how they are categorized, bodhisattvas wish to lead all sentient beings to *nirvāṇa*, so that they no longer suffer the pain of the cycle of birth and death.

When an *arhat* attains enlightenment, their mind enters *nirvāṇa*, but their physical bodies remain and continue to exist. Consequently, the remaining years of an *arhat's* life after attaining enlightenment are called "*nirvāṇa* with remainder." At the end of an *arhat's* physical life, he or she will not be reborn again. This is called "final *nirvāṇa*" or "*nirvāṇa* without remainder." In this way, to "enter *nirvāṇa*" means to put an end to the cycle of birth and death.

Ordinary people often have misconceptions about *nirvāṇa*, especially Chinese lay Buddhists who promote Humanistic Buddhism. Many have heard that the term means "ending the cycle of birth and death," and think, "That's too passive!" It's as if they think "ending" birth and death is selfish, wrong, and goes against the Middle Way. This is not so.

If birth is "coming" and death is "going," then *nirvāṇa* is without coming and going and without birth and death. This is because birth, death, coming, and going are all worldly, illusory phenomena. They are not real. Once you understand the truth of the world, you will discover that nothing truly comes or truly goes. The nature of all things is emptiness. Realizing this truth is *nirvāṇa.*

In the sutras, *nirvāṇa* is as empty, like the open sky. Even though clouds float through it, the sky remains empty. The sky doesn't increase or decrease. Dark clouds do not sully it any more than white clouds purify it. In the same way, once you realize that the world is without coming and going, and without birth or death, the truth of emptiness is not enriched by your realization any more than it is impoverished if you were to remain an ordinary, unawakened person.

After arhats realize the truth of emptiness, their hearts are filled with the exaltation of enlightenment. *Nirvāṇa* is a realm of purity, joy, quiet serenity, and tranquility. They are "full of Dharma joy." Nowadays, many lay Buddhists use the phrase "full of Dharma joy" everywhere, using it to describe ordinary Dharma services or any kind of Buddhist activity. It would be difficult to change that, but these things have nothing to do with what the sutras mean by "full of Dharma joy." You should know that, when the Buddha said "full of Dharma joy" it is an allusion to the bliss of *nirvāṇa.*

Levels of Cultivation

After arising the *bodhi* mind to lead all sentient beings to final *nirvāṇa*, bodhisattvas must develop faith.

First, they must have firm faith in dependent origination, that good causes bring good effects. Second, they must unceasingly perform good deeds, and cultivate merit. Last, they must uphold precepts, cultivate meditative concentration, and see all things with wisdom. The faster they progress in meditative concentration and wisdom, the stronger their faith becomes.

The first teaching bodhisattvas cultivate are the "ten wholesome actions." The ten wholesome actions are an expansion of the five precepts. To improve their physical actions, bodhisattvas refrain from killing, refrain from stealing, and refrain from sexual misconduct. To improve their verbal actions, bodhisattvas refrain from lying, refrain from duplicitous speech, refrain from harsh speech, and refrain from flattery. To improve their mental actions, bodhisattvas refrain from greed, refrain from anger, and refrain from ignorance. Along with cultivating the ten wholesome actions, bodhisattvas uphold the three categories of precepts: the precepts of proper conduct, the precepts for wholesome deeds, and the precepts for benefiting living beings.

From the initial vow to becoming Buddhas, the bodhisattva path can be divided into fifty-two levels. First bodhisattvas traverse the "ten levels of faith." After strengthening their minds of loving-kindness and compassionate vows, bodhisattvas continue on to the "ten levels of dwelling," the "ten levels of practice," and the "ten levels of dedicating merit" (collectively known as the "three degrees of sagacity"). Bodhisattvas who enter the first stage of the "ten grounds," can see all phenomena as empty. This is what people call attaining the fruition of enlightenment.

Chinese Buddhists, whether they are monastics or laypeople, and whether they practice Pure Land, Chan, or Esoteric Buddhism, seem to have developed the idea that enlightenment is beyond their grasp, because it is far too difficult to attain. They think that enlightenment is not something that can be explained in a couple of sentences or understood in a few moments. Let me emphasize: enlightenment is just a matter of seeing the world as it truly is. After seeing the true form of the world, we must continue to cultivate. Cultivating all the way to the final fruition of enlightenment may be difficult, but attaining initial realization is not difficult to do.

Removing Ignorance

If we want to attain enlightenment, we must understand ignorance. Ignorance is located in our *manas* consciousness, which is responsible for sentiment and attachment, most especially the attachment to the self. When we are attached to the self, an enormous portion of our mind and thoughts becomes dedicated to getting what we want. For example, we think of the people we like and how we can see them, or the foods we like and how we can eat them.

Manas Consciousness

Attachment originates from a mistaken view of the self. What we believe to be the self is a combination of the five aggregates of form, feeling, perception, mental formations, and consciousness. The five aggregates change in accordance with causes and conditions. They lack any true, unchanging self-nature. Ordinary people believe that they have a real self, and constantly reinforce this idea. They even believe they have a "self" that has existed in many previous lives, and will continue to be reborn after their present life ends.

The mistaken belief that there is a real, unchanging self is called "ignorance of the self." Ordinary human beings all have this ignorance of the self, which only deepens and becomes more entrenched through attachment, eventually becoming a "view of the self." Because such people believe that the self is real, they develop a deep love for the self and all things related to it, this is called "craving for the self." They compare all that they have with others, and hope to have a self that is better and more powerful than others. This is called "pride in the self."

Ignorance of the self, views of the self, craving for the self, and pride in the self are all part of "self-attachment." They are functions of the *manas* consciousness, and the origin of affliction. In the

Buddha's teachings they are also frequently referred to collectively as "ignorance". The power of ignorance strengthens and develops attachment, leading us to pursue the people and things we like and generate physical, verbal, and mental karma. This is planting the seeds of karma which, in time, will come to fruition. Thus we become trapped in the cycle of birth and death. The main function of ignorance, of the *manas* consciousness, is planting karma and bringing it to fruition.

This process is similar to running a motor. After a motor is started, as long as fuel is continually fed into it, it can keep on running. Similarly the process of growth is genetically encoded into a bean. A bean can lie dormant for long periods of time, but when it is put in water it will sprout. Within our memory we have many impressions accumulated from habits that have lasted for countless lifetimes. This includes happy times, sad times, as well as an enormous number of misconceptions and wrong views. According to the Consciousness-Only School, the impressions from our habits are like seeds and act the same way the seeds of trees, flowers, and grass do. They possess within them all the potential for growth.

If the seeds of these habits do not receive sustenance from external conditions, they will not reach fruition. For example, if the eyes do not look at external sense objects, they cannot be tempted by sights and trigger habits from previous lives. But if the eyes see the right sense objects, the seeds of those habits will sprout and produce joy and sorrow. How we feel about people, events, and things all comes from our experiences from this life or previous lives.

When feelings arise, behaviors and reactions performed in the past may be repeated. Even if a certain behavior has only happened once before, the *manas* consciousness' ignorance of the self, views of the self, pride in the self, and craving for the self drive us to repeat our behavior again and again. We think what we've thought, listen to what we've heard, eat what we've eaten, and do what we've done. Our physical, verbal, and mental actions are driven by these four powers of self-attachment. Once these unwholesome attachments arise in the mind we lose a great deal of freedom.

Suppose you work for a company and made a sizable amount of money. You may wonder, "Should I take the thousands that I made and buy stocks? Should I invest in something? Would it be best to buy an apartment building?"

If you buy the stocks and they plummet, what do you do? No doubt you would experience mental anguish and lose a great deal of freedom. The next time the stocks collapse, you will lose your freedom again and feel the same level of confinement. There are many sources of confinement throughout life that can be called "affliction." Their origin is ignorance—the *manas* consciousness.

Attachment

Plainly speaking, the power of the *manas* consciousness could be called "sentiment." In the sutras, the Buddha talks about *youqing* (有情), "sentient beings," though this can be translated more literally as "those who have sentiment." The ignorant mind of ordinary beings encourages this sentimentality to grow, causing them to become attached to the things they want.

Bodhisattvas are the opposite of sentimental. "Bodhisattva" refers to beings who practice to enlighten themselves and enlighten other sentient beings. They are no longer bound by ignorance or affection. Consider the previous example: if you were to invest in some stocks, your freedom would be limited because of the stake you have in the unstable market. The force that creates this confinement is the sentimental attachment created by ignorance.

Due to ignorance, ordinary beings endlessly think about the people, events, and things they like. This generates mental karma. After thinking such thoughts, they experience impulses to pursue those things and orally express those desires. This generates verbal karma. Then actions arise: they use the internet, phone, or mail to contact the person they wish to see, or make plans to purchase or even steal what they want. This generates physical karma.

The sutras describe sentient beings as "cloaked in ignorance and bound by craving." Craving is likened to a rope within the mind that ties us all about and restrains us with mental knots. Whenever we are near something we like, be it a person, a thing, or a concept, the mind will tie us to it.

When you finish your work for the day or put down the book you are reading, the people, things, and activities most desired will return again to the forefront of your mind. The *ālaya* consciousness stockpiles all these impressions of craving and clinging. When Śākyamuni Buddha discussed the noble truth of the cause of suffering, he said we are "cloaked in ignorance and bound by craving."

The mind is consumed by ignorance, filled with ignorance of the self, views of the self, pride in the self, and craving for the self. The minds of ordinary beings are all like this. When we die, but before we are reborn, our craving and clinging form our *ālaya* consciousness. This compels us to continue in the cycle of birth and death. The noble truth of the cause of suffering can be seen in the twelve links of dependent origination in the links of "ignorance," "craving," and "clinging." These same phenomena are named the *manas* consciousness by the Consciousness-Only School.

Sentiment and Emotion

Ignorance of the self, views of the self, pride in the self, and craving for the self arise from habits in the *manas* consciousness and take their current form. You have heard many times that "All things arise through dependent origination. The Buddha taught that all things are illusory." Even so, if you are robbed, you will still be deeply displeased. This is because your understanding hasn't changed, and you still intuitively believe that "This is mine! Even if it's an illusion, you can't take it from me!"

The feelings of emotion and sentiment that arise from the *manas* consciousness are extremely powerful. They can give you the strength to persevere and never give up, no matter how difficult the task. One example of such a driven, durable person at Fo Guang Shan is Venerable Miao Jin, the head of the Cloud Dwelling Building, where we often hold Dharma lectures. When the construction of the Cloud Dwelling Building was completed and it was still being furnished she accepted the position, directing the workers every day. The task was quite difficult, but she exhibited great determination throughout the process.

When we make trips outside the house, we might find carrying a small handbag to be exhausting. But then we see those mothers who walk with a child in one arm and another on her back. The mothers feel that carrying their children is their responsibility. Because of this, they do not feel the least bit tired. They adore their children, so they feel satisfied.

This sentimental connection between parents and children is incredibly powerful. It cannot be severed. It only grows stronger as children grow, driving parents to work hard to support their children. Sentient beings, *youqing* (有情), are "those with sentiment." But this sentiment can also develop in an unwholesome way, causing people to go out into the world and cheat, steal, and harm others. In more severe cases, they may even kill others.

How can we prevent unwholesome sentimental attachment from developing? First, we can restrain our speech and actions by upholding precepts. If the mind desires what it can't have, we can use meditative concentration to control those thoughts of desire. When we have a strong foundation of upholding precepts and cultivating meditative concentration, we can use our wisdom eyes to see all things as illusory.

The *Heart Sutra* says, "Thus, in emptiness, there are no forms, feelings, perceptions, mental formations, or consciousness. No eye, ear, nose, tongue, body, or mind." This encourages everyone to examine how each of these sense organs arises through dependent origination. They are not real or unchanging, for they lack self-nature. Whatever we hear, see, taste, or whenever sense contact occurs, we must return to the power of meditative concentration.

They do not have an unchanging and actually existing physical nature (they lack self-nature). Whether it is heard, seen, tasted, whenever sensual contact has occurred, it is essential to turn back to one's power of concentration. One must immediately observe that this is not real, that this is false. This is called "the cultivation of wisdom.

Theravāda Buddhism commonly divides the path of practice into three parts: morality, meditative concentration, and wisdom. This is also a way of grouping the different parts of the Noble Eightfold Path: morality encompasses right speech, right action, and right livelihood. Meditative concentration encompasses right effort, right mindfulness, and right meditative concentration. Wisdom encompasses right view and right thought. These three categories can also be found among the six perfections from Mahāyāna Buddhism as the perfection of morality, the perfection of meditative concentration, and the perfection of wisdom. Since wisdom is ultimately the factor which grants liberation, why is it necessary to cultivate morality and meditative concentration?

Before ordinary beings fully develop *prajñā*-wisdom, most continue to repeat their past mistakes, believing that all things are real. A longstanding meditation practice can help us discern external sense objects and internal thoughts with greater clarity. Whatever we encounter we can think at once: "This is not right. This is wrong. This is not real." These are realizations.

After these realizations, it is still possible to use the sentiment of the *manas* consciousness to take care of things. However, after such realizations our ignorance of the self, views of the self, pride in the self, and craving for the self will have been removed by wisdom. Right view and right thought can be used to cure the illness of ignorance. "Realization" is recognizing the truth of the world. However, the true meaning of being a bodhisattva is to use sentiment to liberate sentient beings, without leaving a single one behind.

The Wisdom of the Diamond Sutra

Those who wish to study Mahāyāna Buddhism should learn what the world is really like and afterwards begin to practice. To succinctly describe the world we can say two things: it is impermanent, and it is produced through dependent origination. Because the world is impermanent, all things arise, abide, change, and cease. Since the world is produced through dependent origination all things arise through a combination of two or more causes and conditions.

For example, tables, houses, and other material objects are all created from more than two component parts that are arranged into a structured form. Then even the water we drink is H2O: two parts hydrogen, one part oxygen. In order to get beansprouts, which contain water as well, people used to place dry beans in bags until the temperature and humidity became right for them to sprout. Alfalfa sprouts are grown in the same way.

All things and events take shape through dependent origination, and arise in accordance with causes and conditions. Nothing lasts forever. As the doctrine of dependent origination states: "When this arises, that arises. When this exists, that exists." Nothing is real, fixed, or unchanging. Everything is empty.

The *Diamond Sutra* describes all worldly phenomena as illusory, existing for only a brief time. The sutra says they "are like dreams, illusions, bubbles, and shadows." Why? Because anything that arises is certain to break down and vanish. To return to alfalfa sprouts as an example: once they run out of water they begin to wither. They exist for only a short amount of time. Fruit is ripe and delicious for only a short period of time, then begins to rot. That is why all things are called illusory.

The same can be said for human beings. People live twenty, thirty, fifty, or perhaps even one hundred years. But in the end they all perish. Turtles live even longer, but in the end, they also die. Everything in the world is continually changing. Nothing is permanent.

Perhaps you might say, "Many animals have short life-spans, so it is easy to see them as impermanent. But it is difficult to appreciate the impermanence of inanimate things like steel." Consider how the earth revolves around the sun: the earth is traveling through space over one hundred times the speed of sound. It travels more than a thousand kilometers a minute, but we cannot feel it. Strange, is it not? There are clouds of gas in our solar system that move even faster, but we cannot feel their speed either. Even if we do not directly experience it, all sentient beings and all insentient things are subject to impermanence just the same.

Four Wrong Views on Cause and Effect

The great Buddhist philosopher Nāgārjuna Bodhisattva examined the logic behind different systems of causation and non-causation to prove how all phenomena arise through two or more causes and conditions. Some of the possible models of causation he refuted are listed below:

1. Arising Without Causes
This refers to the idea that phenomena can arise anywhere, for no logical reason, without any cause or condition. For

example, suppose a fire starts in some area, then a fire could start anywhere for seemingly no reason. That's not how things are in reality. Even if we cannot yet discern any reason for the fire, there must be some cause. And any subsequent fires would require causes as well.

Some other ancient Indian religions believed that phenomena could arise spontaneously in this way, without need for cause and effect. As such, they believed that the rich would remain perpetually rich and the poor would remain perpetually poor. But if we follow this logic, aren't all human endeavors meaningless? Additionally, if we observe the world closely we can see that this explanation doesn't hold up. Thus "arising without causes" is a wrong view.

2. Self-Arising

Since phenomena do not arise out of nowhere, we can conclude that they must have some kind of causes and conditions. Still, there are many different hypothetical possibilities for how phenomena arise. Some examples refuted by Nāgārjuna are "self-arising," "external-arising," and "collective arising." The first of these, self-arising, refers to phenomena which arise with themselves as the cause.

If phenomena were only dependent on themselves as a cause, that would mean that they do not change: before they are self-arisen and after they are self-arisen would be the same. For example, if a certain thought arises in the past, if it were self-arisen then it would arise just the same again in the future. If the mind were self-arisen and not affected by outside conditions, then it would only give rise to the same thought again and again.

But our thoughts are changing constantly. Whenever the six sense organs make contact with the six sense objects, different thoughts arise. Those who are cultivating meditative concentration should train themselves to focus intently on a meditation object. But to keep the mind steady and focused, it requires consistent practice. Thus, "self-arising" is inconsistent with what we see of causes and conditions.

3. External-arising

While some people see how "self-arising" is not sensible, they believe in a sort of "external-arising," in which phenomena arise from outside causes, but that there is no specific relationship between cause and effect. With this view, any cause can generate the same effect. But if this were true, cows could give birth to horses, as could hens, or dogs. If this were true, just as wood can be burned for fire, so could water or iron.

Some people may think, "Buddhism says that all things arise depending on càuses and conditions. But we aren't born from 'causes and conditions,' we're born from mom and dad!" Think of things this way: is a father alone sufficient to give birth to a child? Could a mother alone become pregnant? There must be two or more qualifying factors for a child to be born. And even so, do the bodies of either parent exist independently? They too are made up of causes and conditions. All things are a part of an interrelated web of mutual reliance, repeating the process: "When this arises, that arises. When this exists, that exists." There are no people, events, or things that are fixed, unchanging, and real. All are empty and endlessly changing. This is the truth that the Buddha awakened to.

4. Collective Arising

Some people see how "self-arising" and "external-arising" are not sensible and think that a combination of the two, "collective arising," may work. Perhaps phenomena arise through both ways: self-arising in some aspects and externally-arising in others. Combining false theories in this way also doesn't work. Suppose there was a blind man on a journey who could not see the road in front of him— if there were three blind men on the same journey this would not increase their ability to see that road.

Each of these views is unworkable. What we observe instead is this: causes lead to effects, and a specific combination of factors must be present to generate a specific effect. This is dependent origination. All things arise depending on causes and conditions. They do not arise on their own, and if a certain cause or condition is changed the resulting effect changes as well. No state can be preserved forever, and all things lack a true and unchanging substance.

Take this body as an example: it is composed of the four great elements of earth, water, fire, and wind. The earth element represents stability, like our skeleton and muscles. The water element represents cohesion, like blood, water, and urine. The wind element represents movement, like the breath. The fire element represents ripening and separation, like the heat in the body.

Plants and minerals are also made up of the four great elements. For example, something lit on fire will burn to a cinder: this is separation. When preparing food, fire causes things to be cooked and "ripen." Fruit trees grow and flower depending on their surrounding climate, and this too is "ripening" through fire. Through analysis we can see how each of the four great elements arises from causes and conditions. All of the elements are continually changing, lacking a single essence. This is akin to the line from the *Heart Sutra:* "Form is not different from emptiness, emptiness is not different from form."

Our mental composition is much the same. Within the five aggregates, the last four are all mental functions: feeling, perception, mental formations, and consciousness. "Feeling" is dependent on contact to occur before feelings arise. "Perception" also depends on contact for words and concepts to arise. "Mental formations" depend on perception before deliberations and decisions can be made. According to the Consciousness-Only School, the "consciousness" aggregate is composed of the mind consciousness, the *manas* consciousness, and the *ālaya* consciousness. All mental functions arise depending on causes and conditions. They do not arise on their own, and therefore do not have real, substantive form.

The Consciousness-Only School divides the functions of the consciousness into categories: the five sense consciousnesses, the mind consciousness, the *manas* consciousness, and the *ālaya* consciousness. The five sense consciousnesses are the neurological functions derived from bodily sensations after the eyes, ears, nose, tongue, and body have come into contact with external sense objects. The mind consciousness performs the mental functions of contemplation, reasoning, determination of preferences, and decision-making. The *manas* consciousness performs the functions of self-attachment, as explained earlier, while the *ālaya* consciousness contains the impressions of many lifetimes of physical, verbal, and mental behavior.

Do not assume the *ālaya* consciousness we carry lifetime after lifetime is permanent and unchanging. Do not think that it is an independent entity. What we do, think, and say throughout the course of our many lives leaves impressions of those behaviors. They are added to the great storehouse that is the *ālaya* consciousness. For this reason, it is also subject to endless change. Physical behavior, mental behavior, and the outside world all arise in accordance with dependent origination, and all are empty.

The Diamond Sutra on Emptiness

Once we see that the five aggregates that make us up are empty, we can then see that the five aggregates that make up other people are empty too. The *Diamond Sutra* says, "Thus by liberating infinite, immeasurable, limitless sentient beings, in reality, no sentient beings are liberated."

If you think about this passage you may say, "That's totally backwards! First it says that all beings are liberated, then it says that no beings are liberated. That's a complete contradiction!" However, bodhisattvas see that their five aggregates are empty. In the same way bodhisattvas can see the five aggregates that make up you, me, him, or her are the same: form is not different from emptiness, emptiness is not different from form. Once the notion of a self is gone, the notion of others is also eliminated.

The appearance and lifespan of sentient beings is also not real. As the *Diamond Sutra* says, "No notion of sentient beings and no notion of longevity." The four notions are all empty. As bodhisattvas liberate sentient beings, they discover that sentient beings are not real and unchanging entities. According to the *Diamond Sutra*, "All sentient beings are not sentient beings." That is why it states that "In reality, no sentient beings are liberated."

This does not apply only to human beings. All material things arise through a combination of causes and conditions. They are also not real. For example, if I accidentally knocked my alarm clock off my bed stand and onto the floor, it would break and the various parts of the clock would be strewn about. The plastic frame would go back to being a plastic frame, the screws would go back to being screws, and the springs would once again just be springs. Without being gathered together as an alarm clock, the pieces lose their collective functions. In this way, both the existence and the function of the alarm clock are temporary. When we examine things through dependent origination, we see that all people, events, and things can be thought of as a combination of two or more factors. When these causes and conditions separate, the forms that arise from them change. Their prior states no longer exist. All states are empty. They are temporary and not real.

The line from the *Diamond Sutra* that "All phenomena are illusory" applies both to sentient beings and insentient things. The *Āgamas* say, "To see dependent origination is to see the Dharma. To see the Dharma is to see the Buddha." This means that if you want to see emptiness, you must examine how all worldly phenomena take shape and disappear according to dependent origination. Realization comes from seeing that arising and ceasing, coming and going, wholesome and unwholesome, pure and impure, and good and bad are all impermanent, not real, and illusory.

In the Chan School there is an expression: "See your true nature and become a Buddha." This describes the abovementioned thought process and seeing Buddha nature. Everyone should try to find an opportunity to attend a meditation retreat, or at least attend a short session of sitting meditation. We shouldn't imagine that, "One day I'll be sitting in meditation and then 'Bam!' I'll be enlightened." Enlightenment is gained through contemplation. As the *Śūraṅgama Sutra* says, "Entrance into *samādhi* is gained through the wisdom of hearing, thinking, and practicing." The Chinese Chan Buddhism also incorporates elements of Consciousness-Only philosophy, stressing that wondrous existence is found in true emptiness. As such, the methods of cultivation are a bit different than what was explained previously.

The Diamond Sutra on Dependent Origination

To have insight into impermanence means to understand that everything arises through dependent origination. Thus all things are unreal and illusory. The latter half of the *Diamond Sutra* focuses on removing wrong views while liberating sentient beings. For example, the sutra discusses removing the misconception that all things truly exist. The *Diamond Sutra* says that adornment is not adornment, and that that is what is called adornment; that the world is not the world, and that that is what is called the world; that sentient beings are not sentient beings, and that that is what is called sentient beings. While we as bodhisattvas adorn the Pure Land and teach sentient beings, the mind must also understand that there are no sentient beings to teach. Enlightened beings are fully equip with wisdom eyes that see emptiness and Dharma eyes which see phenomena clearly in all their detail for the sake of liberating sentient beings. But even though bodhisattvas see all things, there is nothing to be seen. A bodhisattva sees that mountains are not mountains, and lakes are not lakes. They know that all things are illusions which arise through dependent origination, and thus are not real.

Since long ago, we have taken all people, events, and things to be real. Thus we abide in them mentally. For example, if you have some item of value and knew that others wished to take it by force, your mind will be consumed by it. You will refuse to show the item to others. This is "abiding" in something: giving something frequent attention and hanging your mind upon it. This is the same as being cloaked in ignorance and bound by craving

Ordinary, unenlightened people allow the mind to abide in things, especially the people, things, states they like. The practice of not abiding in anything mentioned in the *Diamond Sutra* means not forming attachments to people, events, and things. The sutra teaches us to examine whether such things truly exist or not. We should engage in spiritual cultivation, while at the same time we should not believe that spiritual cultivation possesses a real and unchanging nature.

The Diamond Sutra and the Middle Way

After the line, "Thus by liberating infinite, immeasurable, limitless sentient beings, in reality, no sentient beings are liberated," the *Diamond Sutra* goes on to say, "If a bodhisattva has the notion of a self, the notion of others, the notion of sentient beings, or the notion of longevity, then he is not a bodhisattva." "He is not a bodhisattva" means that such a person is not a highly cultivated bodhisattva, and would not be a true practitioner.

The *Awakening of Faith in Mahāyāna Treatise* mentions two classes of practitioners: "those of great understanding" and "true practitioners." A person of "great understanding" refers to someone who has an intellectual understanding of emptiness, but has not yet had an initial realization. A "true practitioner" is a bodhisattva who has such a realization and thus has eliminated self-attachment and the notion of self. With no notion of self, they liberate sentient beings and allow them to understand emptiness and the meaning of *nirvāṇa*. At the same time, they know that "no sentient beings are liberated." This is the mind that does not abide in anything. This is the Middle Way as expressed in the *Diamond Sutra*.

Liberating Sentient Beings

The *Diamond Sutra* says that bodhisattvas "should give rise to a mind that does not abide in anything." Previously I explained what it means to "not abide in anything." Now I will explain what it means to "give rise to the mind." The *Diamond Sutra* describes the practice of great bodhisattvas. Bodhisattvas cultivate the six perfections:

Giving, morality, patience, diligence, meditative concentration, and wisdom. In previous chapters I have explained meditative concentration and wisdom at great length, and explained diligence via the "four right efforts." Below I will explain the remaining three perfections: giving, morality, and patience.

Perfection of Giving

The *Diamond Sutra* says, "A bodhisattva should practice giving without abiding in anything." This means that, as a bodhisattva liberates sentient beings, they should not only give money, goods, and medicine, but that their generosity should extend to their own bodies, bones, marrow, and whatever else sentient beings need for liberation. Bodhisattvas should also understand that such things are not real. This is why the *Diamond Sutra* says, "This means that he should not give abiding in form, nor should he give abiding in sound, smell, taste, touch, or *dharmas*."

Bodhisattvas should give others confidence, give others joy, give others hope, and render service to others at all times. Every day we have opportunities to give rise to a mind that does not abide in anything. One way is to realize the emptiness of the "three spheres:" the giver, the recipient, and the gift.

Consider the gift itself as an example. The paper a dollar is made of can be used to make many different banknotes. Depending on what country the currency is from and what denomination, it will feature different historical figures' portraits, designs, and carry different values. Also, as the economy changes the value of a given note changes with inflation and deflation. Even the exact same banknote can change in buying and selling power over time. Since the money we give changes in accordance with the causes and conditions of the world, it does not have a fixed value. In this same way, all the things we give are not truly real.

Consider now the giver and the recipient, like when a person gives a stick of sugarcane to an elephant: both the person and the elephant are made of the five aggregates, all of which are empty. What the sutra calls "giving rise to a mind that does not abide in anything" is accomplished when we can give and know that the giver, the recipient, and the gift are all empty. This is the "emptiness of the three spheres."

If the mind does not abide in anything while giving, we will attain great merit. How great? The *Diamond Sutra* uses measuring the size and extent of space in every direction. Can you even imagine how vast that is? A bodhisattva who practices the six perfections without abiding in any notion will attain merit as unimaginably vast as space. When a bodhisattva uses a compassionate heart and the wisdom of emptiness to cultivate, whether they give material things or Dharma, their merit and wisdom will be like emptiness itself. This is cultivating merit and wisdom together, and is the only means by which one can attain Buddhahood.

When we give with a mind that does not abide in anything, we will have no obstacles. Suppose a person gives you a gift with a mind that abides in something, he may think "You completely forgot about the ten dollars I gave you last time!" When you two meet again and greet each other, he may think, "Last time I gave him quite a bit of money and now he can't even be bothered to acknowledge me." Or perhaps two people treat each other well, but often criticize each other. In this situation, someone is liable to start holding a grudge. Or suppose someone lays himself on a line for another, but is not rewarded for the effort. All of these can create mental discomfort, because the mind is abiding. It is split between opposing views, and not free. If a bodhisattva with this kind of mind tries to liberate sentient beings, he will certainly encounter obstacles.

A mind that sees the three spheres as empty is the supreme *bodhi* mind. The merit of cultivating such a mind far, far exceeds the merit of ordinary people. The *Diamond Sutra* often compares the two. For example, the *Diamond Sutra* says that reciting, explaining, and upholding the teachings of its four-line verse can grant great merit. In another passage from the sutra, the Buddha states that if every grain of sand in the Ganges River became a world, and all those worlds were filled with gifts of the seven treasures, the merit of practicing the teachings of the sutra would still be greater than the merit of such a gift.

It is even said that the merit of a person who practices giving throughout as many lifetimes as there are grains of sand in the Ganges River is only one to one ten-thousandth the merit of those who explain and uphold the teachings of the *Diamond Sutra* or its four-line verse for the benefit of others. Why is this? No matter how many material things we give, they still have limitations. But the gift of the Dharma allows people to attain enlightenment and become Buddhas. In this way, the merit of giving Dharma is boundless.

Perfection of Morality

The *Diamond Sutra* first explains the perfection of giving and moves onto the others. The remaining perfections of morality, patience, diligence, and meditative concentration are all grounded in *prajñā*-wisdom. Together they encourage us to give rise to a mind that does not abide in anything. For example, the perfection of morality cannot arise when the mind abides in something. If a bodhisattva feels that he or she is very moral, then that bodhisattva would view others as undignified. From this the bodhisattva would be engaging in differentiation and arrogance.

People become annoyed at the very sight of an arrogant person. People may say, "Hey! So you are a decent, moral person, but I'm not, huh?" Those who are more blunt may say, "So you're the only one who gets to claim a moral high ground? The rest of us do not uphold the precepts, is that what you're saying?" If people find you arrogant, they will avoid you, and you will lose the necessary causes and conditions to liberate them.

Liberating sentient beings has always occurred with kindness, gentleness, encouragement, and consolation. When a person is arrogant, even when he gives, others will not want to receive his gifts. Even if they must accept the gift for some reason, they do so uncomfortably. They may reluctantly accept in order to survive but promise themselves that, "I won't accept anything from him ever again!"

When it comes to morality, bodhisattvas who do not abide in anything do not compare or count their merit against others. People who just practice morality on their own don't enumerate their merit or hold themselves as superior to those who do not abide by the Dharma. The sutras say that, "One principle that bodhisattvas should adhere to is that, when encountering immoral people, treat them with even greater sympathy and care." You should know that, just as spiritual cultivation is not easy for you, it is the same for all people. Who can claim to have never done wrong? For this reason we should have sympathy for others, comfort them, and guide them. This is the perfection of morality.

Perfection of Patience

Sometimes when we interact with others communication can be difficult, creating a lot of affliction. To excel at networking, social interactions, and relationships, keep in mind the following: When criticizing a person's faults, do not do so in public or in front of a large group of people. When praising a person's positive qualities, find a location with as many people as possible.

When you are wronged, criticized, misunderstood, attacked, pressured, or insulted in public, you should control the mind with *prajñā*-wisdom. Have no notion of self and no notion of others.

Otherwise such abuse will be hard to bear. With *prajñā* wisdom, even if someone schemes against you, traps you, or makes you miserable, you can ignore it. Without disputing such things you can remain indifferent and unaffected by them.

You should go as far as to compliment your enemies in front of others. Think about it: Do you have the ability to be wronged and still cultivate? Can you pull it off? Only those who have eliminated self-attachment can do so. Those who have not eliminated self-attachment have great hatred for their enemies and think, "I've already held my tongue toward him. Now you want me to praise him? No way!"

The teachings of the *Heart Sutra* and *Diamond Sutra* are intimately related to our lives. For there to be harmony in human relationships, self-attachment must be eliminated. This is difficult to achieve. But to succeed is to be a true bodhisattva. For example, sounds arise through dependent origination. Consequently, there are no absolutes to determine if a sound is good or bad. Like someone striking a table with a bang, the sound quickly disappears. Whether criticism or praise, both are like the bang of a table: they are transient, fleeting, and do not linger after they are gone.

Whether someone says, "Wow! What you said is amazing!" or, "You're such a jerk!" your words will fall silent within a moment. They are not real. If we think of things this way we will no longer care about the opinions of others. What would life be like if we did not have the wisdom of the *Diamond Sutra*?

Suppose someone walks by, sees your haircut, and blurts out, "Wow! That looks awful!" For that person it is a casual remark that is immediately forgotten. But you may suddenly find yourself needing to run to the mirror and fiddle with your hair. Instead you should remind yourself, "I should give up the notion of a self anyway." Otherwise, you will end up obsessing over what other people say about you all day. That's not worthwhile, is it?

Venerable Master Hsing Yun often remarks, "Where there is Dharma, there is a way." Such a saying arises from *prajñā*-wisdom. We should place our faith in cause and effect, that "good begets good and bad begets bad." Believe that, in the end, good intentions will no doubt be rewarded. Trust in this and you will be able to persevere until the very end. If we look at things from an even broader perspective, though all things accord with dependent origination, they are also are empty of any self-nature. Does anything truly exist? With this in mind, we can be less prone to haggling, more moral, and more patient. When we liberate sentient beings, no obstacles will impede your way.

The *Diamond Sutra* extols the benefits of upholding its teachings, but admits that those who do may still be "disdained by others." Though we suffer disdain, we can do so without quarrelling with others. This is because we can reflect upon *prajñā*-wisdom and have no notion of self and no notion of others. In this way we can endure any attack or slander. This truly is a great form of spiritual cultivation.

Even after attaining this realization, we still must continue to cultivate, just as before. Each day we continue to uphold precepts, not harm others, and maintain a singularly focused mind. In addition, we contemplate the emptiness of the four notions, so that we have no notion of self, no notion of others, no notion of sentient beings, and no notion of longevity. All four relate back to "non-self," and support the *Heart Sutra's* injunction to "realize the five aggregates are empty."

1. No Notion of Self
When people insult you for no reason, this is when you need wisdom the most! You should recall that "form is not different from emptiness, emptiness is not different from form," and quickly remember to have "no notion of self,

no notion of others, and no notion of sentient beings." In this way you can avoid being upset by an insult. If you are able to do that, it is a sign that your self-attachment is weakening. The focus of the perfection of wisdom sutras as a whole is to eliminate self-attachment, and in the *Diamond Sutra* this is called having "no notion of self."

2. No Notion of Others and No Notion of Sentient Beings

When the *Diamond Sutra* says to have "no notion of others," it is indicating that the concept of "others" is illusory. Everyone walks, thinks, and talks. This is the "notion of others." As another example, cows walk around on four hooves, eat grass, drink water, and moo. This could be called the "notion of cows." It is possible to have a notion of every sort of animal. But all sentient beings are a combination of the five aggregates, and thus are empty.

3. No Notion of Longevity

When the *ālaya* consciousness enters a mother's body, through the stages birth, maturity, old-age, sickness, and death, this makes up a life. In the *Diamond Sutra*, it is referred to as "notion of longevity." If we have no notion of self, how can we have the notion of longevity? How long a human is on the earth is also an illusion. Once we realize that these four notions are empty, we gain the ability to withstand any and all insults, slander, and attacks.

The *Diamond Sutra* largely discusses emptiness. Why then does the sutra say, "If those good men and good women who receive, uphold, read, and chant this sutra are disdained by others, it is due to negative karma incurred in a former life... Eventually his negative karma from previous lives will be eradicated, and he will attain *anuttara samyaksambodhi*." This passage shows that when we face adversity, frustration, and abuse in our lives, these instances are removing our self-attachment.

With this thought, all frustrations become tolerable. This is not the kind of tolerance where you clench your teeth and think, "Forget it! It doesn't matter." Instead, this tolerance uses *prajñā*-wisdom and sees the five aggregates as empty. In this manner, every instance of practice strengthens our right view. Once we fully attain right view, we can successfully contemplate the emptiness of the self, allowing us to live at ease.

Eliminating our habits is only possible through *prajñā* wisdom. This is especially true of the habit of self-attachment. Meditative concentration can give us the power to control our thoughts, so that we do not wildly form attachments to many things. The wisdom of being without the four notions is to continually work toward removing the ignorance of self, views of the self, pride in the self, and craving for the self which exist in the *manas* consciousness. We pursue this endeavor until we attain freedom and liberation.

The *Diamond Sutra* teaches us to be without the notion of a self. No matter how many times we recite the name of the Buddha or bow to Buddha images, these remain superficial efforts. Even if we cultivate meditative concentration and contemplate emptiness, we should not take pride in these practices. Why? The *Diamond Sutra* addresses this issue specifically:

> "Subhuti, what do you think? Would it be right for a *srotapana* to think like this: 'I have attained the fruit of *srotapana*'?"
>
> Subhuti said, "No, World-honored One. And why is this? *Srotapana* means 'stream-enterer', and yet there is nothing to be entered. To not enter into form, sound, smell,

taste, touch, or *dharmas* is what is called *srotapana.*"

"Subhuti, what do you think? Would it be right for a *sakradagami* to think like this: 'I have attained the fruit of *sakradagami*'?"

Subhuti said, "No, World-honored One. And why is this? *Sakradagami* means 'once-returner', and yet in truth there is no such thing as returning. This is what is called *sakradagami.*"

"Subhuti, what do you think? Would it be right for an *anagami* to think like this: 'I have attained the fruit of *anagami*'?"

Subhuti said, "No, World-honored One. And why is this? *Anagami* means 'non-returner', and yet in truth there is no such thing as never returning. This is the reason it is called *anagami.*"

"Subhuti, what do you think? Would it be right for an *arhat* to think like this: 'I have attained the path of an *arhat*'?"

Subhuti said, "No, World-honored One. And why is this? There is no phenomenon called '*arhat*'. World-honored One, if an *arhat* were to think 'I have attained the path of an *arhat*', then he would be clinging to self, others, sentient beings, and longevity.

Someone who says, "I have achieved a certain state" verifies their continued self-attachment. This is not to say that practitioners should not be concerned with the progress of their practice. But it is important to avoid the pitfall of feeling well-cultivated and sanctimonious. When among sentient beings, practitioners should be able to lower their guards and act casually. Practitioners who feel they are superior to others and believe they are remarkable still have self-attachment. The *Diamond Sutra* describes this attitude as abiding in something. Abiding in enlightenment or that status of being enlightened is still abiding.

The *Heart Sutra* emphasizes self-cultivation. It teaches us to realize that everything is empty, all conditioned phenomena are impermanent, all phenomena lack self-nature, and that *nirvāṇa* is perfect tranquility. In the Noble Eightfold Path this is called "right thought," and is also called the "*prajñā* of contemplation" in Mahāyāna Buddhism. In both instances, it is using the wisdom of emptiness to build a proper outlook on life. Everything we do should be approached with right view. Only through direct experience with life can we have right view. In this way the *Heart Sutra* teaches Humanistic Buddhism.

The *Diamond Sutra*, on the other hand, emphasizes practicing as a bodhisattva. It teaches us to give rise to the *bodhi* mind and to practice the six perfections and four means of embracing. These practices are necessary to liberate all sentient beings and bring them to final *nirvāṇa*. This is the ultimate form of great compassion. From one's initial vow all the way to attaining *bodhi*, we should clearly know the true form of phenomena. This is the wisdom of emptiness shared by all bodhisattvas. The *Diamond Sutra* is the complete application of Humanistic Buddhism, and can be taken as a reverent treatise on how to practice as a humanistic bodhisattva.

Chapter Twelve

LEAVING A MEDITATION RETREAT

Practicing Humanistic Buddhism means understanding that all things within the world are illusory while peacefully abiding among the world with its sense objects in the here and now. Through these efforts we can distance ourselves from the five desires of wealth, sex, fame, food and drink, and sleep, and remove the five hindrances of greed, anger, sloth, agitation and remorse, and doubt. Those who cultivate meditative concentration should not long for the future or yearn for the past. The future is uncertain, and what is there in the past we can return to?

The *Diamond Sutra* says "The mind of the past cannot be obtained, the mind of the present cannot be obtained, and the mind of the future cannot be obtained." In life, only those who can see through, let go of, and remove their own discrimination, attachment, arrogance, jealousy, and dissatisfaction can remove the notion of a self, or, going a step further, remove the notion of others or the notion of sentient beings. With no notions, such people are unimpeded wherever they go.

After you leave the meditation hall, it is essential to continue cultivating attentively in your ordinary life. When we are around others is the best time to use the skills gained in meditation. Of course, it is still necessary to constantly hone your abilities in seated meditation. Only in this way can you apply the Buddha's teachings in your daily life.

Guarding the Sense Organs

The sutras tell us to closely guard our sense organs. Of the six sense organs, the eyes are most likely to give rise to thoughts of discrimination and produce affliction. "Closely guarding the sense organs" means to cautiously take care of one's eyes, ears, nose, tongue, body, and mind and not allow them to come in contact with desirable sense objects. Next, train yourself to be moderate in eating and drinking, to be dedicated to wakefulness, and have a mind that is content and detached. Through these efforts you will reduce your afflictions as much as possible.

When leaving the meditation hall and returning to ordinary life you will be faced with all manner of long-winded chatter and insipid speech, and you will overhear plenty of talk that is unhelpful and does not accord with the path. You should do all you can not to add to this kind of talk. When you are with others, remember: follow conditions as they arise, but ensure that the mind is steadfast and unchanging. Develop a mind that cares for its own thoughts as they arise and change, practices moderation, and leaves worldly things far behind. To "leave things far behind" does not mean being distant from others. When people engage in self-indulgent chatter, rumor-spreading, or meaningless banter, do not join or interrupt them. These are the things we leave far behind.

Abiding in Right Wisdom

After leaving the meditation hall, it is essential to continue practicing seated meditation. Once you have developed meditative concentration, you will be able to brighten the mind such that you can retain clarity with every thought. You will act clearly knowing good and bad, right and wrong, and proper and improper. In this way, practitioners control their body, speech, and mind. Living in this way is called "abiding in right wisdom."

Right wisdom is a state of great awareness. A mind imbued with right wisdom can maintain brightness and clarity at all times. Only a mind steeped in meditative concentration can develop right wisdom and use its power to subdue affliction. There are times when the allure of external sense objects is strong, or the mind gives rise to affliction. At such times we may be unable to subdue desires and impulses. This is a sign of an unfocused mind.

Though you fully know that you should not be thinking, speaking, or doing something, you may lack the mental strength to be in control. When you come across a favorable sense object, the mind becomes irrepressible and thinks about it unceasingly. When an unfavorable sense object is merely mentioned, anger arises and yet you won't stop thinking of it. A person such as this has insufficient *prajñā*-wisdom and lacks right view. At times like this it is important to remember wise passages from the sutras, such as "All forms are illusory," "All conditioned phenomena are like dreams, illusions, bubbles, or shadows," and "No eye, ear, nose, tongue, body, or mind; no form, sound, smell, taste, touch or *dharmas*."

In the sutras, *prajñā*-wisdom is often compared to a sword, because it can effortlessly cut through affliction. This is especially true of moments where there is a conflict between emotion and wisdom. Such conflicts create ambiguity and hesitation. This is where *prajñā*-wisdom is most useful. Practitioners who lack the foundation for wisdom will frequently have petty arguments with others, because they do not practice with the thought that the five aggregates are empty, and that all worldly phenomena are empty. They have not developed the skill, and are not yet committed.

Conclusion

The more the outside world tests us, the more it becomes a place of cultivation, and the better it becomes at guiding us to develop right view. The outside world helps us confirm the usefulness of *prajñā-* wisdom. When we encounter adverse conditions, we must learn to create the causes for beneficial conditions. To walk the path of Humanistic Buddhism without obstruction, we must train ourselves. When encountering sense objects, we should direct our attention inward. Use *prajñā-*wisdom to interact with people, events, things, the five desires, and other such matters. Only by severing affliction and eradicating ignorance can merit and wisdom be perfected.

> To practice, one must rely on oneself,
> And frequently attend meditation retreats.
> What can remove all affliction?
> Mahāprajñāpāramitā.

After a meditation retreat is over, each person walks away with some benefit. Nevertheless, after leaving the meditation hall, it is essential that they continue to practice diligently in their daily lives. Within a meditation hall, we cultivate in stillness. Once we interact with people again we must learn to cultivate in activity. Spiritual cultivation requires simultaneously upholding precepts, cultivating meditative concentration, and developing wisdom. We must simultaneously advance in hearing, thinking about, and practicing the Buddha's teachings. This is a singular, undeniable truth of Buddhism. Let us all continue to train diligently!

List of Texts

Venerable Master Hsin Ting extensively quotes the Buddhist sutras throughout his teachings, often sharing short passages from a staggering variety of works. If a reader is moved by a particular passage, the next step of visiting the literature itself can be a difficult one. An alphabetical list of sutras is provided below to assist in this process. The sutras are organized by their titles in English, except in such cases when the Sanskrit name of the text has become commonplace, as in the case of the *Dharmapada*. Each text is also listed with its common Chinese title, both in Chinese characters and pinyin pronunciation.

Amitabha Sutra
    Amituo Jing   阿彌陀經

Awakening of Faith in Mahayana Treatise
    Dacheng Qixin Lun   大乘起信論

Connected Discourses
    Za Ahan Jing   雜阿含經

Contemplation [of Infinite Life] Sutra
    Guan Wuliangshou Jing   觀無量壽經

Diamond Sutra
    Jingang Jing   金剛經

Eight Realizations of a Bodhisattva Sutra
  Ba Daren Jue Jing   八大人覺經

Flower Adornment Sutra
  Huayan Jing   華嚴經

Fundamental Verses of the Middle Way
  Zhong Lun Song   中論頌

Great Treatise on the Stages of the Path to Enlightenment
  Putidao Cidi Guang Lun   菩提道次第廣論

Heart Sutra
  Bore Boluomiduo Xin Jing   般若波羅蜜多心經

Lotus Sutra
  Fahua Jing   法華經

Mahaprajnaparamita Sutra
  Bore Jing   般若經

Original Vows of Ksitigarbha Bodhisattva Sutra
  Dizang Jing   地藏經

Surangama Sutra
  Lengyan Jing   楞嚴經

About the Publisher

Buddha's Light Publishing offers quality translations of classical Buddhist texts as well as works by contemporary Buddhist teachers and scholars. We embrace Humanistic Buddhism, and promote Buddhist writing which is accessible, community-oriented, and relevant to daily life.

Founded in 1996 by Venerable Master Hsing Yun as the Fo Guang Shan International Translation Center, Buddha's Light Publishing seeks to continue Master Hsing Yun's goal of promoting the Buddha's teachings by fostering writing, art, and culture. Learn more by visiting www.blpusa.com.